Sādhus

DOLF HARTSUIKER

Sādhus
HOLY MEN OF INDIA

Inner Traditions
Rochester, Vermont • Toronto, Canada

The jewel is lost in the mud,
and all are seeking for it;
Some look for it in the east,
and some in the west;
some in the water and
some amongst stones.
But the servant Kabir has appraised it
at its true value,
and has wrapped it with care
in the end of the mantle of his heart.

Rabindranath Tagore, *Songs of Kabir* [1]

Inner Traditions
One Park Street
Rochester, Vermont 05767
www.InnerTraditions.com

Copyright © 1993, 2014 by Dolf Hartsuiker

Designed by Maggi Smith

Library of Congress Cataloging-in-Publication Data
Hartsuiker, Dolf, author.
  Sadhus : holy men of India / Dolf Hartsuiker.
     pages cm
  Reprint. Originally published: 1993.
  Includes bibliographical references and index.
   ISBN 978-1-62055-402-9 (pbk.)
   ISBN 978-1-62055-414-2 (ebook)
 1. Sadhus—India. I. Title.
 BL1241.53.H37 2014
 294.5'61—dc23

                                    2014008720

Printed and bound in China by Toppan Leefung Printing Ltd

10 9 8 7 6 5 4 3 2 1

Names of Sādhus on the cover.
Front Bola Giri.
Back Bajrang Dās.

Frontispiece Mādhav Dās in front of his humble dwelling, built against the ancient city walls of Dwarka. He is said to be a hundred years old, but this should be taken as an expression of respect, reflecting a culture where old age is equated with wisdom.

pp. 4–5 Prayāg Giri, a Nāgā Bābā, has made his temporary shelter at Gomukh ('cow-mouth'), the source of the holy Ganges, where the icy water flows out of the Himalayan glaciers. For six months he will worship the goddess Gangā Mā (Mother Ganges) and serve the pilgrims who come here for her darshan and a holy dip.

pp. 12–13 Bābās stand on the edge of the holy Shipra, their flower garland offerings already afloat, awaiting a signal to enter the water.

Contents

ॐ नमो नारायण

Om namo Nārāyana

'Om, salutation to Nārāyana'

Preface

When I visited India for the first time, I stayed for a year and travelled all over the subcontinent, fascinated and bewildered by the total 'otherness' of Hindu culture, the magic of its living religion, the wisdom of its philosophy, and the architectural marvels of its splendid heritage – feelings that contrasted with my dismay at the poverty and misery prevailing in large parts of the country. I have returned many times, for long periods, and the 'magic' is still there – in certain places. It is not yet submerged by the deluge of gross materialism and conspicuous consumerism that is swamping the West, and which is now heading East as well.

In the perplexing confusion of India, a foreigner would at first hardly notice its 'holy men', mystics and ascetics: the Sādhus, as they are collectively designated. Although there are four to five million of them, it took me several voyages to differentiate them from the surrounding overload of strange, beautiful, ugly, magical, brutish, spiritual impressions. They do not constitute more than about half a percent of the total population. Moreover, although Sādhus can be found all over India, they usually live in far-off places and a little hidden from everyday life.

Of course, I knew of a few singular, famous 'Gurus' who were preaching in the West, but like most fellow Westerners, I had never heard of Sādhus. Somehow their presence seems forgotten, though they have been known to the West since at least 300 BC, first as the 'naked philosophers' when the Greeks visited India, and later by European travellers as the 'fakirs'. However, in the popular image of India and even in Indological studies, their existence – fundamentally shaping Hinduism since remote antiquity, and 'living' it today – hardly plays a role.

When I first met with Sādhus, I was amazed, even a little frightened, by their powerful and earthly 'otherworldliness', which seems a paradox and is not at all comparable to the pious, humble holiness of Christianity. I admired their choice of a free life, without possessions, comforts, sensual pleasures – and responsibilities. But above all, I was struck by their beauty.

I wanted to record it before it vanished, before the Sādhus became extinct in this increasingly consumerist and secular world. I'm a bit more optimistic now, having seen their vitality, knowing that they have survived the millennia and various adverse invading cultures. Nevertheless, change seems inevitable – and probably for the worse. Besides, there were

'Camera yoga' at the Kumbha Melā in Ujjain.

more than enough reasons to photograph them, one being that, strangely enough, nobody had ever systematically done so.

On my photographic quest I visited many holy places, attended religious festivals, and encountered and photographed thousands of Sādhus. With some Sādhus I became closely acquainted and over the years met them time and again; with most, quite naturally, I had more superficial contacts.

It soon became apparent that in order to understand what I was seeing and photographing, it was necessary to study the available litera-ture on Sādhuism – which is not as extensive, thorough and detailed as one would hope for – and on the wider cultural context. Needless to say, the subject matter is vast and complex, though extremely interesting, and even now, having spent years in India and in studying its culture, I cannot say that I have seen the end of it. To really comprehend it all demands a lifetime, or better still, leading the life of a Sādhu oneself.

I thank all Sādhus for their *darshan* and *āshirvād*, and all my friends for their cooperation and support.

Dolf Hartsuiker

आदोल्फ्

*Find the eternal object of your quest
within your soul.
Enough have you wandered during the
long period of your quest!*

*Dark and weary must have been the
ages of your searching in ignorance
and groping in helplessness;*

*At last when you turn your gaze
inward, suddenly you realize that the
bright light of faith and lasting truth
was shining around you.*

*With rapturous joy, you find the soul
of the universe, the eternal object of
your quest.*

*Your searching mind at last
finds the object of the search within
your own heart.*

*Your inner vision is illuminated by this
new realization.*

Yajur Veda 32.11

1 Inner Light

Enlightenment is the real purpose of life. That is still the basic concept of Indian culture, in which mystics, who devote themselves to the full-time exploration of the 'inner light', are very highly respected.

The 'inner light' is the core of one's consciousness and is identical with or part of the Absolute, the Cosmic Consciousness, though that is unknowable to the ordinary human mind.

The intellect, trying to picture what cannot be grasped, or – if it has been able to 'see' – trying to express what can only be approximated in the language of mortals, must resort to symbolism, art and poetry.

> *He who knows the first vital thread,*
> *binding all the things formed in shape,*
> *colour and words, knows only the*
> *physical form of the universe, and*
> *knows very little.*
>
> *But he who goes deeper and perceives*
> *the string inside the string, the thin*
> *web binding separate life-forces with*
> *cords of unity, knows the real entity.*
>
> *Only he knows truly the mighty*
> *omnipotent and omnipresent Brahman,*
> *Who is within and beyond all*
> *formulated entities of the vast universe.*[2]

The Brahman, understood as 'the Absolute', is the highest, the most abstract and the least comprehensible God, and is therefore generally approached through personal deities one level lower in the pantheon. This consists of thousands of gods and goddesses, but the most important are Brahmā the Creator, Shiva the Destroyer and Vishnu the Preserver.

Opposite Rupa Nāth, a Gorakhnāthī of the Aughār subsect, sits in front of a shrine in Pashupatinath (Nepal), which is not only a place dedicated to Shiva, but also a centre of Gorakhnāthīs. (For more on the Shaiva sects, see p. 48 onwards.)

Although Brahmā is the head of this holy trinity, in practice only Shiva and Vishnu, and their various manifestations and incarnations, are worshipped. These two divine personalities represent different philosophical and religious traditions and consequently possess very diverse characteristics. Hinduism can thus be divided into Shaivas – the devotees of Shiva – and Vaishnavas – the devotees of Vishnu.

Holy Men

Professional mystics are collectively known as 'Sādhus'. In their pursuit of the 'inner light', the liberation from all earthly bonds and the 'knowledge' of the Absolute, they have chosen the way of asceticism and yoga. This implies a systematic 'reprogramming' of body and mind by various methods, such as celibacy, renunciation, religious discipline, meditation and austerities. The general term given to these methods is *sādhanā*, literally 'the means of achieving a particular goal', from which the word 'Sādhu' is derived.

The Sādhus are regarded as holy men, representatives of the gods. Like Shiva and Vishnu, and just as diverse in their manifestations, they are the outcome of a long and varied history.

The use of asceticism and yoga as metaphysical science and mystical method to re-establish the link between the individual soul and the Absolute, or rather to 'realize' their fundamental unity, seems to be a unique Indian invention, the first evidence of which can be traced back about 4500 years.

There is, however, some dispute over the exact time and place – and thus culture – of its origin. Some scholars conjecture that asceticism was implicit in the teachings of the holy Vedas, which came to India with the 'invasions' of the Āryan tribes around 1500 BC, and that the early ascetics were dissenters from an increasingly ritualistic Vedic religion.

The other theory, seemingly supported by archaeological evidence, is that asceticism and yoga originated in the Indus Valley culture, which was already fully developed in 2500 BC, and that these methods evolved out of earlier shamanistic practices.

The 'Horned God'

The archaeological evidence of ascetics in the Indus valley culture consists mainly of steatite seals, several of which depict a 'horned god' who has been identified as the prototype of god Shiva – as the King of Yogīs and as the Lord of the Animals – because of his resemblance to the image of Shiva in later Hinduism.

He is called the 'horned god' because of his headdress, which consists of two buffalo horns and an unidentifiable upright form in the middle. This whole configuration resembles the trident, or *trishūl*, the characteristic weapon of Shiva. The 'deity' is seated in a variant of the lotus posture, or *padmāsana*, which is the typical way of sitting of all *yogīs* and emblematic of Shiva as King of Yogīs. A very striking feature of the 'horned god' is his erect penis, which resembles numerous later depictions of Shiva in various manifestations, and which could also be related to the ubiquitous aniconic representations of Shiva as the *linga*, his erect phallus. Furthermore, the 'deity' has three faces, a characteristic found in many later iconographic representations of Shiva as the trinity Shiva–Vishnu–Brahmā. Finally, he is surrounded by wild animals, which is typical of Shiva as Pashupati, the Lord of the Beasts.

Besides these seals more cult objects have been found: the so-called ringstones and phallus-shaped stones, which may be regarded as prototypical symbols of the *yoni*, the female generative organ, and the linga. These finds therefore could be further proof of the existence of a proto-Shiva deity in the Indus Valley culture, or at least of a cult centred around the worship of the generative organs as symbols of fertility and creation.

There is some controversy regarding the interpretation of these archaeological finds, notably of the 'horned god',[3] which may not be solved until a major obstacle to a conclusive understanding – the inability to read their script – has been removed. No doubt even then controversy will remain, for 'in dealing with ancient Indian gods any theory is necessarily based on some more or less subjective predilection for viewing things from a special angle and for emphasizing particular facts and connections.'[4]

The Indus Valley culture, already in decline, seems to have come to an abrupt end as a result of the Āryan invasions – or rather was 'submerged' under this dominating culture. Nevertheless, parts of it survived and resurfaced, including asceticism, the worship of the linga, and the proto-Shiva, which were within a few centuries incorporated into mainstream Hinduism.

The identity of asceticism as originally an indigenous – for the Āryans 'alien' – practice is further evidenced by the early Vedic scriptures' ambivalence and even hostile disapproval towards the ascetic, matched by their contempt for the aboriginal phallus-worshippers.

This of course represents the view of those who compiled these scriptures, the upper-caste *brāhman* priests, descendants of the conquering Āryans; they dominated the weaker tribes – eventually to become the lowest castes – and looked down on the strange religious practices of those 'barbarians' and their ascetics. For Āryan society contrasted sharply with the aboriginal societies it conquered: it was materialistic and hedonistic.

This does not mean that the Āryans were without any mystical inclination. The holy scriptures of their conception were clearly inspired by the transcendental experiences of the *rishis*, the 'seers'. These experiences, however, were not induced by any extreme asceticism, but rather by drinking a mysterious psychotropic substance called *soma*, the 'nectar

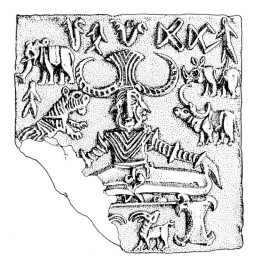

Seal depicting the 'horned god' (actual size 31 mm × 31 mm).

of immortality'. Their mystic message formed only a small part of an increasingly over-elaborate system of rituals, primarily aimed at propitiating the gods through sacrificial offerings for materialistic ends.

The brāhman priests controlled the fire sacrifice, which formed the quintessence of Vedic religion and was originally proclaimed as the only way to please or to coerce the gods. But gradually the 'alien' ascetic and religious practices of the aboriginals were recognized as equally powerful.

An interesting myth illustrating the incorporation of asceticism into mainstream Hinduism concerns the fire sacrifice of the rishi Daksha, of good Āryan stock, about to take place on a mountaintop in the Himalayas. All the gods and their consorts have been invited, except Shiva and his wife Pārvatī. They have been deliberately excluded since the sacrifice is dedicated to Vishnu, the Vedic sun god, who is regarded as the sole Supreme Lord.

Shiva is not acceptable in this illustrious company because of his filthy, 'polluting' habits: he runs around naked in the jungle; keeps the company of wild beasts, goblins and ghosts; covers his body with ashes from the cremation grounds; uses a skull as a drinking cup; is continually intoxicated by the use of hashish; and acts like a madman, laughing wildly. He is a black magician, a Tantric, an ascetic of the Left Hand path, in short, an outsider.

Shiva's wife is terribly insulted and wants to take revenge. Shiva tries to calm her down by remarking that his disciples are worshipping him with the true meditative spirit for which no fire sacrifices are needed, but this does not mollify her. Eventually giving in to her rage, Shiva approaches the company of gods in his terrible form as the God of Destruction, with fire blazing forth from his third eye, and threatens to destroy them all. Intimidated by this show of force, Daksha has to admit his mistake – 'better his anger than the blessings of other gods' – and subsequently worships him as the most powerful god, without whom the fire sacrifice would not be complete.

In this myth two kinds of fire are shown: the 'outer' fire of the sacrifice, which is the Vedic way to reach the gods; and the 'inner' fire of Shiva, created by his ascetic practices, the non-Āryan way. It was Shiva's fire against the sacrificial fire, and Shiva's prevailed.

Shiva eventually became one of the dominant gods in the pantheon, and asceticism was institutionalized as the last and culminating stage of life for the 'twice-born'. Moreover, mysticism and asceticism as a full-time occupation came to be accepted and even admired.

The 'twice-born' belong to the three highest castes: the brāhman priests; the warrior and ruling class; and the trader and merchant class. The 'once-born', the *shūdras*, were later designated the 'menial class', but at first consisted of the subjugated aboriginals, the prisoners of war.

The 'twice-born' should devote the first stage of life to study of the scriptures as a celibate student (*brahmachārī*) under the guidance of a Guru. The second stage is the productive, procreative life of the householder (*grihastha*), fulfilling his duties to family and caste. In the third stage he must retire to the jungle, where he may be accompanied by his wife, and lead the chaste life of a forest hermit, performing the fire sacrifices and reciting the scriptures. In the fourth and final stage he must renounce all and become a wandering ascetic, a *sannyāsī*, and seek union with Brahman.

The Long-haired Sage

The characteristics of the early ascetics, holy men and sages, as these can be inferred from the Vedas and subsequent holy scriptures, are quite similar to those of contemporary Sādhus: they were naked and wore long hair in matted strands; their bodies were covered with dust or ashes, or with rags, bark or animal skins; they painted marks on the forehead and body, and carried a staff and a water vessel; they practised celibacy, some forms of yoga and bodily mortifications; and they lived in forests, aloof from the society of mortals.

These holy men are beautifully portrayed in the 'hymn of the long-haired sage'.[5]

> *The long-haired one carries within himself fire and elixir and both heaven and earth. To look at him is like seeing heavenly brightness in its fullness. He is said to be light himself.*
>
> *The ascetics, girdled with the wind, are clad in brownish dust. They follow the path of the wind when the gods have entered them.*
>
> *'Intoxicated by our austerities we have ascended to the higher planes. You mortals see just our bodies.'*

A version of the 'austerity of fire'.

*The ascetic flies through the air, illuminating all forms below.
Given to holy work he is the companion of every god.*

*Air is the only food of the god-inspired, and the ascetic is at
home in both worlds, the spiritual and the material.*

*Wandering in the track of celestial nymphs and sylvan beasts,
the long-haired one has knowledge of all things, and with his
ecstasy inspires all beings.*

*The Wind god churned it, and ground it, then the long-haired
one drank the elixir from the vessel, together with Shiva.*

The 'elixir' in the first and last stanzas is evidently some kind of psychotropic substance, in all probability related to soma, the Vedic sacrificial
libation offered to the gods and taken to induce visions of divine Reality.
But, as the first stanza indicates, it may be present in the body as well,

either created or augmented by ascetic practices. The same reasoning applies to the 'fire within', the inner 'mental heat'. Through his austerities the long-haired sage even becomes the 'fire', enlightening all around him.

In the second stanza, 'girdled with the wind' implies 'naked', which has later been called *digambar*, or 'sky-clad'. The 'brownish dust' is the prototype of, or analogous with, the ashes that naked Sādhus have applied for centuries, and which they still do today.

'Intoxicated' in the third stanza refers to a state of ecstasy or 'divine madness' due to god-realization, effected by the elixir or by austerities. This intoxication is also contagious; the mere presence of the ascetic may transmit it, as is indicated in the sixth stanza.

The supernatural powers of the ascetics described in the fourth and fifth stanzas, 'flying through the air' and 'living on air', were taken quite literally, and distant echoes of these magical feats even reached the West, as for instance 'The Hindu Magician floating in the air' depicted in the fourteenth-century *Livre des Merveilles*, or Book of Marvels (overleaf).[6]

Apart from the supernatural feats described in the hymn, these ascetics exhibited another, more 'natural', miracle, that is, keeping the penis erect without any sexual sensations or intentions.[7] This yogic achievement is no doubt related to the aboriginal worship of the phallus, and to the 'horned god' and other images of Shiva with his linga raised. In all probability the ascetic's erect linga was worshipped as well, until at least the seventeenth century (see Picart's engraving, pp. 24–25).

Bearers of Skulls

Before the ninth or tenth century AD the ascetics had no discernible organizational structure. However, for at least two thousand years there had been many different groups of ascetics united around a realized sage or Guru, distinguished by their particular tradition and an unbroken line of religious preceptors, by their faith toward a particular deity and religious doctrine, and by their habits, rules and appearance.

Some of the earliest sects were the Pāshupatas, the Kāpālikas, the 'bearers of skulls', and the Kālāmukhas, or 'black-faces'. Derived from Pashupati, the Lord of the Beasts, the name Pāshupatas indicates that this sect may be related to the 'horned god' of the Indus Valley culture. They traced their descent from Lakulīsha, a manifestation of Shiva, who closely resembles the 'horned god' with a very distinct erect phallus.

These ascetics worshipped Shiva in his terrifying manifestations as Bhairava, the licentious ecstatic 'madman' (see p. 34), or as Kapāleshwar, the Lord of the Skull. Shiva gained this last epithet after having chopped off the fifth head of Brahmā, which then became stuck to his hand. To expiate his crime – and get rid of the skull – he had to perform severe austerities.

The Kāpālikas emulated their Lord of the Skull in doing voluntary penance, though they were not necessarily guilty of any murder. The following, rather sympathetic, description of one Kāpālika Sādhu called

'The Hindu Magician floating in the air'

Bhairavācārya, meaning 'Bhairava-teacher', would probably fit most of these ascetics.[8]

> [Bhairavācārya was] seated on a tiger-skin, which was stretched on ground smeared with green cow-dung, and whose outline was marked by a boundary ridge of ashes. The flashing lustre of his body was like red arsenic paste, purchased by the sale of human flesh. His long hair was twisted together in ascetic fashion and was festooned with rosary beads and shells. He had a slanting forehead mark, made with ashes. He wore a pair of crystal earrings, and constant at his side was a bamboo staff with a barb of iron inserted in the end. He had observed the vow of celibacy since childhood.

> [One day he performed a powerful spell at] the empty house near the great cremation-grounds, on the approaching fourteenth night of the dark fortnight. In the centre of a great circle of ashes white as lotus pollen, Bhairavācārya could be seen, seated on the breast of a corpse that lay supine and had been anointed with red sandal and arrayed in garlands, clothes and ornaments, all of red. Arrayed in a black turban, black unguents, black amulet and black garments, he had begun a fire rite in the corpse's mouth, where a flame was burning. As he offered some black sesame seeds, it seemed as though in eagerness to become a Vidyādhara ['possessor of knowledge'] he were annihilating the atoms of defilement that caused his mortal condition.

This was in fact a rather 'civilized' ritual, since the Kāpālikas practised human sacrifices as well. Bhairava was a thirsty god, who had to be appeased with offerings of wine and blood, animal or, preferably, human. The flesh and blood consecrated to the deity were consumed by the ascetics – a primeval Eucharist – in order to induce mystical union.

A logical progression from the sacrifice of other bodies is sacrificing one's own body. This may range from penance and discipline to austerities, mortifications, self-mutilation, and ritual suicide. So it is reported that Kāpālikas, apart from their 'normal' austerities, cut off pieces of their own bodies and used these as sacrificial offerings.

Besides these macabre rites, they were engaged in severe *hatha yoga* exercises. However, their primary objective was not to attain mystical union with the deity, but to acquire magical yogic powers, such as clairvoyance, becoming invisible, entering someone else's mind, walking on water, and flying through the air.

Needless to say, these sects were condemned and rejected by the brāhman priests and respectable society. Nevertheless, at a later stage, when their extremist practices had mellowed a little, they acquired a wide following.

The brāhman priests were not too happy either with two other ascetic organizations, the Buddhists and the Jains. These 'heretics' rejected the Vedas as an infallible source of knowledge and condemned animal – let alone human – sacrifices, recognizing the existence of a soul in all living beings. This is expressed by their concept of *ahimsā*, or 'non-injury', which was only much later incorporated into Hinduism.

Overleaf The artist Picart, who made this engraving in 1729, had to depend totally on the information of the traveller Tavernier, who had witnessed the scene over sixty years before and had some sketches made on the spot. Nevertheless, its accuracy is remarkable and the 'penitences', with some minor discrepancies, resemble those of today: 'keeping the arms raised', 'standing', hatha yoga, 'fire austerities' and 'suspended animation in a grave' (here erroneously depicted as a sarcophagus). On the extreme right is an intriguing scene. Drawn with a certain modesty, but no lack of essential detail, it shows a woman kissing the ascetic's penis. As Tavernier observed, the ascetics thus worshipped receive these reverences without showing 'any sign of sensuality, but on the contrary, without regarding anyone, and rolling the eyes terribly; you would say they are absorbed in abstraction.'[9]

2 Shiva

Shiva, the 'auspicious', first appears in the scriptures as an epithet of Rudra the Vedic storm god, who had to be placated in order to deflect his ferocious temper, and who is therefore euphemistically addressed as *shiva*-Rudra, 'auspicious Rudra'. By the second century BC Shiva had acquired a separate identity, usurping many of Rudra's fierce characteristics, and he continued to grow in importance. Numerous folk deities and lesser gods were absorbed by him, adding to his stature and creating a complex, even paradoxical deity, as is reflected in his 1008 names, all representing different facets of his personality.

Eventually he was elevated to the highest position in the Hindu pantheon, forming part of the trinity Brahmā–Vishnu–Shiva as the god of Destruction. He is not a brutal annihilator, but, like a forest fire preparing the ground for new vegetation, he destroys and re-creates, as these two life processes are inseparable and complementary. In this 'terrible' aspect he is Hara, the 'seizer', representing death and sleep; and he is Mahākāla, the Great Timekeeper, calculating the aeons and leading all things to final dissolution.

The God of Destruction
Shiva's favourite technique of destruction is by fire: his 'inner fire', accumulated as a result of his extreme asceticism. It blazes forth from his third eye, since Shiva is the Three-eyed Lord. His left eye represents the moon and his right eye the sun. These two are his worldly eyes, directed outwards. His third eye, situated in the middle of his forehead, is usually directed inwards and is then the eye of Knowledge or Discrimination. When directed outwards it may become the eye of Destruction, incinerating his antagonists: personified or deified egotism, ignorance, greed, lust and apathy.

Fire from his third eye burns up Kāma, the cupid god of Love – or rather Lust – as he is about to shoot his flowery arrow at the meditating

---

Opposite Sukh Deva is clothed in a very bright red, the colour of Shiva, associated with the orange-red of fire, or the dark red of sacrificial blood. Like many Shaivas he carries a *trishūl* (Shiva's 'weapon of Destruction'), to which a *damaru* (Shiva's 'drum of Creation') is attached.

A popular devotional print depicts Lord Shiva in his auspicious form: he meditates amid paradisiacal scenery, his eyes half-closed in divine bliss, alone at the heart of the infinite. Shiva's long, magical hair, his *jatā*, is reputedly the seat of his powers, while the crescent moon on his forehead, the cobra around his neck, the river Ganges, and the full moon identify him as a fertility deity. Shiva's nakedness epitomizes his primal state, his non-attachment to the world, while the soft, feminine contours of his body represent his transcendence of opposites. He is covered with ashes, symbolic of death and regeneration.

Shiva for the express purpose of annulling his yogic powers. Shiva's dominance was envied by the other gods, who had therefore sent Kāma to distract him with love.

> When Shiva was about to dance, his eye-fire
> reducing the sun to a lustreless circle
> with its flames that yellow the faces of the quarters
> threw out before him
> a stage-curtain of hot light.[10]

Much symbolism has become attached to Shiva's flaming trident, the trishūl, which is well equipped for this purpose since so many metaphysical concepts are threesomes. Mythologically the trishūl is a weapon for the destruction of evil, but back in the Stone Age it was no doubt conceived practically, as a real weapon.

Living in the jungle, as ascetics continued to do even after the rest of humanity started to live in agricultural communities, necessitated the use of a weapon – and of fire – for warding off wild animals, who were not so impressed by the ascetic's holiness as popular folk tales suggest. Even in quite recent times the trishūl was still used as a lethal weapon, for ahimsā, the principle of 'non-injury', was a fairly late addition to the ascetic belief-system.

Another word for Nāgā ('naked') is *digambar*, which would literally translate as 'sky-clad'. Usually, however, the Nāgā Bābās are dressed in more than just 'sky'. Shiv Nārāyana Giri for instance wears many *mālās* and even a crown of the *rudrāksh* beads characteristic of Sādhus devoted to Shiva.

Mahant Rāmeshwar Giri's face and body are embellished with very elaborate *tilak*. In his left hand he holds a peacock-feather whisk, with which he lightly touches the faithful in blessing; near his right hand stands a bowl with sweets, to be distributed as *prasād*, holy food. In front of him on his tiger-skin *āsana* are some coins and notes, donated by devotees.

There are many different designs, in varying sizes, of different metals, from crude self-made jobs to very ornate professional castings. The primeval trident was evidently made of animal horns and was probably related in symbolism to the headdress of the 'horned god', the proto-Shiva. Even today this type is found, as is shown by the trishūl made of real horns on page 88. But after the invention of copper casting the animal horns were replicated in the new metal alloy, a very practical improvement, which really turned the trident into a lethal weapon and simultaneously emphasized its symbolic meaning – notably its solar aspect. For copper is, next to gold, a 'solar' metal.

As this relation is explained mythologically, the trishūl is made of brilliant filings of the sun. The middle prong represents lightning or the sun. The crescent shapes of the outer prongs, the horns, are identified with the waxing and the waning moon, a prominent symbol in Shaiva iconography, as evidenced by the crescent moon in his hair, emblematic of rebirth and regeneration.

The God of Creation

In the trinity Shiva's 'official' function is the Destroyer; nevertheless, his role as Creator is much more emphasized in the popular imagination, and he is depicted as such on posters and calendars decorating the walls of many homes, shops and offices. In this function he reveals himself as the ancient Pashupati, the Lord of the Beasts, who later acquired the duty of 'Herdsman' – not only of the domestic animals, but of people as well.

In one of his creative manifestations, Shiva is Natarāja, the King of the Dance, perpetually performing the Cosmic Dance in a ring of flames.

Effortlessly equalling the Brahman, in meditational bliss, he is the Unmoved Mover, hidden in animate and inanimate objects like fire in wood, and makes them dance with his power. His left foot is raised, and with his right foot he crushes a struggling dwarf, the personification of delusion, desire and sloth. He is four-armed, denoting his omnipotence, and in one of his left hands burns the flame of Destruction. With one of his right hands he rattles the drum of Creation, the *damaru*. It produces the primordial sound, the rhythmic pulsing that is the origin of creation. In harmony with his voice, this sound is the source of all music, all language, all knowledge.

The *linga* is the aniconic representation of Shiva, his erect phallus, the symbol of divine procreation and fertility. One of the earliest known Hindu sculptures is a Shiva-linga that leaves no doubt about its phallic character, precisely detailing the glans atop the shaft.[11] Its antecedents go back to pre-Vedic times, when there were various cults of phallic worship, and not only in the Indus Valley. As an object of worship it is more often found in Shiva's temples than his anthropomorphic image, and it is estimated that there are at least thirty million lingas.

The first linga was created by Shiva when Brahmā and Vishnu had a heavenly quarrel about their relative importance and they asked him to intercede. Shiva did not argue with them but appeared in a huge pillar of light, and said: 'He who shall be able to find my beginning and end shall be deemed superior.' Both tried very hard for a long time but failed.[12]

ॐ नमः शिवाय

Om namah Shivāya

This pillar of light is called the *jyotir-linga*, and nowadays there are twelve lingas that are recognized as representing the original.[13] The oldest of the lingas have existed since time immemorial and are considered 'self-originated' and not manmade. The 'self-creation' and discovery of these miraculous lingas are the stuff of legends. Although every village would claim their linga to be 'self-originated' and thus most holy, there are only sixty-eight lingas that qualify. All the others are made by man, according to very strict rules about shape, dimensions and proportions.

Paradoxically, Shiva is both the deity with his 'organ raised' and he is Yogī-rāja, the King of Yogīs, who has renounced sexuality. Alternating in his mythological roles as the lover of Pārvatī, his wife, and as the jungle hermit, he is the erotic ascetic. This ambiguity can partly be explained by his historical expansion from minor deity to major god, all the while absorbing qualities from the 'outmoded' deities, who subsequently diminished in importance.

This ambivalence also reflects the basic yogic connection between the virile force and spiritual power: the flame of sexuality, which has to be fanned by austerities, feeding the bonfire of mystical ecstasy. Shiva's seed, as a rule, is not spent; the seed is 'raised upwards' like his linga, which remains swollen with all potential future creations.[14] Like all great gods, Shiva is the *coincidentia oppositorum*: he is Creation and Destruction, he is the Lover and the Yogī; in his person all dualities are contained, resolved and transcended.

The Great Goddess

Shiva's female counterpart is Shakti, whose name stands for 'divine female power or energy'. She is the Great Goddess, Mahādevī, the final amalgam of the many fertility and earth goddesses who predominated in the matriarchal civilizations of pre-Vedic and non-Āryan India. The relationship between Shiva and Shakti therefore dates back to their infancy, but did not become a source of inspiration – and speculation – in the scriptures until much later. The goddesses were only reluctantly admitted in the patriarchal Vedic pantheon and even then usually as consorts of the gods, deriving their function and power from them.

The goddesses were accepted as powerful divinities in their own right only in those areas that remained longest outside the Āryan sphere of influence, where they tended to dominate the gods. It is not surprising, therefore, that in those areas the *shākta* cults, who worship Shakti in one of her manifestations, came earliest to fruition and subsequently influenced all of Hinduism, gaining recognition for such great goddesses as Durgā and Kālī.

Opposite Mahant Saraswatī Giri gives *darshan*, 'exhibits' himself, in a rather provocative pose. His nudity however is not at all erotic. It shows rather that he is beyond sexuality.

Sādhu Charan in front of his hut of rough stones and sackcloth. His forehead and arms are adorned with the three-striped emblem of Shiva, painted in sacred ashes. He stares at the sun and with his posture seems to connect the solar energy with the earth, letting the divine light flow through him.

Kālī has many aspects in common with Shiva. She is the goddess of Time (*kāla*) and thus Creation and Destruction. But whereas Shiva is usually portrayed in his auspicious aspect, she is depicted in her most ferocious manifestation. She is *kālī*, black as the night; her emaciated body is naked except for a girdle of cut-off arms and a garland of severed heads; in her four hands she holds a noose, a sword, a blood-filled skull and a severed head; her blood-red tongue hangs out of her mouth with fang-like teeth with which she devours all beings; and she has three eyes, tinged red, intoxicated. She consumes her own offspring, but still she is the Mother Goddess. It is clear that whoever wants to get close to the Mother must first conquer the fear of death.

In her relation with Shiva she is the dynamic, energizing principle, and he is passive, receptive. As the saying goes: 'Shiva without Shakti is *shava*, a corpse.'

This is often depicted as the very much alive Kālī standing over the bloodless supine body of Shiva. In a variant on this theme, Kālī is

Rāma Samundar Giri lives in a small hut between the memorial stones at the cremation grounds. An excellent place for the realization of the transitoriness of life, a place where Shiva himself might sit in meditation.

Overleaf Lakshmī Nārāyana Giri, dignified in his simplicity and poverty, obeying the ascetic precept of possessing no more than the absolute necessities, resides temporarily in front of a Shiva shrine at Pashupatinath in Nepal, where he has come to celebrate the yearly festival of Shiva-rātri.

squatting over Shiva and having intercourse with his seemingly uncon-
scious body, which nevertheless shows full phallic capability. This kind
of sexual symbolism is most representative of the metaphysics of the
shākta cults.

The *shāktas* are related to the much earlier Kāpālikas who worshipped Shiva–Bhairava, but in contrast they focus on the goddess, for
to them Shakti represents the real power. A pivotal part of their rites was
ritual copulation. This explicit sexual variant of Shakti worship is some-
what derogatorily designated as the 'left-handed way', the left hand being
the 'bad', impure hand. When these rites were properly executed, the
shaktas would worship the goddess in their female partner, who for the
moment was Shakti incarnate, and experience divine fusion and heavenly bliss. Evidently, this ritual was not always performed in the correct
spirit, but used as a façade for promiscuous sexual indulgence.

The shākta cults that survived the centuries increasingly emphasized
the 'right-handed way' – publicly at least – which represents a sublimation of the original practice, enacting the divine fusion in contemplative
imagination. The rituals, inner processes, supernatural relations and so
on were still expressed in explicit sexual terms, but these were interpreted
as metaphors, and as such have left their traces in rites of worship, metaphysical terminology, mythological imagery and hatha yoga 'physiology'.

'That art thou'

The early ascetics were predominantly devotees of Shiva, and they were
divided into various cults and sects, many of whom were, from the
brāhman point of view, engaged in objectionable practices. Shankara,
a religious reformer of respectable descent, therefore set out to convert
these ascetics and to establish an organizational structure of ten subsects
and four monastic centres. His conversion efforts were rather successful,
but nevertheless quite a few 'aberrant' sects and cults held to their own
views and continued in various forms – evolving or degenerating – up to
the present.

Shankara, respectfully called Shankarāchārya, the suffix *āchārya*
meaning 'teacher', is assumed to have lived around AD 800. His biog-
raphies, which were written a long time after his death, differ in details,
but in general it can be deduced that he was regarded as an incarnation
of Shiva – Shankara, the 'auspicious one', is one of the epithets of Shiva –
and took to the life of an ascetic at the age of eight. He travelled widely,
visited all the holy places and centres of learning, and whenever he met
ascetics or sages with a different philosophy, he would hold a debate and
win them over to his point of view through his logical and lucid exposi-
tion of the scriptures, notably his interpretation of the Vedānta, the 'end
of the Vedas', a collection of philosophical works appended to the Vedic
literature. He left the body at the age of thirty-two, having accomplished
a lasting revitalization of Hinduism.

Luxuriant hair, beautiful *jatā*. Most Nāgās let all hair grow, but some, like the Bābā on the right, radically shave it all off, which is the only other option.

The name – Mast Giri – of this Nāgā Bābā refers to divine 'intoxication' (*mast*) and he certainly looks it: his bloodshot eyes are as those of Lord Shiva in his 'mad', terrifying aspect. Yet how gentle he is.

Shankara's philosophical system has become known as Advaita Vedānta, or 'pure monism', the cardinal tenet of which is: 'Brahman alone is real, the world is unreal and the individual soul (*ātman*) is no other than the Universal Soul.'[15] In other words, *tat tvam asi*, 'That art thou'.

> *As the sparks from the well-kindled fire,*
> *In nature akin to it, spring forth in their thousands;*
> *Living beings of many kinds go forth*
> *And again return into him.*[16]

Brahman is pure existence, consciousness and bliss, devoid of all attributes and all categories of the intellect, and therefore unknowable: 'Brahman is not this, Brahman is not that.' When associated with potency (*shakti*) and illusion (*māyā*), he appears as the qualified Brahman, and is then known as Brahmā, who is the creator, preserver and destroyer. The material world is thus a transformation and expression of the essential nature of Brahman: he is both in the world and above it.

Shankara emphasized that from the phenomenal point of view the world is quite real – so long as true knowledge has not dawned – and that māyā is not pure illusion, but rather absence of knowledge and wrong knowledge. The individual is ignorant of the essential unity of ātman and Brahman, and it is only through realization of this unity that the veil of māyā is lifted.[17]

The wise, yearning for freedom, should therefore renounce all transitory things, bear all afflictions with forbearance, control the sense-organs, accept the true teachings of the scriptures and the Guru, and fix the mind on one goal: *samādhi*, which is the realization of Brahman.

The Ten Names

Of equal importance were Shankara's organizational activities. By establishing a structure for the hitherto scattered Shaiva sects, he created a counterforce to the spreading of Buddhism and Jainism, which by then were already fully organized. This ascetic organization became known as the *dashnāmīs*, or 'ten names', referring to its ten divisions. The 'ten names' each have a traditional meaning, which should somehow reflect the qualities of their members:

Giri	(mountain) the serenity and steadiness of a mountain
Purī	(city) perpetual communion with Brahman
Bhāratī	(learning) blessed with learning
Vāna	(forest) living in the woods
Āranya	(forest) living in forests, free from attachments
Pārvata	(mountain) like Giri, living in mountains
Sāgara	(ocean) possessing the depth of the ocean of truth
Tīrtha	(river-crossing) realization of the highest Self
Āshrama	(hermitage) above the pleasures of worldly life
Saraswatī	(true knowledge) through sounds, tunes

The ascetics of these orders are called *sannyāsīs*, 'renouncers', or more specifically *dashnāmī sannyāsīs*, and they add the designation of their particular brotherhood as a suffix to the name they receive from their Guru during initiation.

Apart from the majority of regular sannyāsīs some special types are distinguished, such as the *dandīs*, the *brahmachārīs*, the *viraktas* and the *Nāgās*. The dandīs are those who carry a stick, a *danda*, which from time immemorial has been the distinction of the master. Only those belonging to the caste of brāhmans have this privilege. Caste differentiation is also noticeable in the composition of the ten sects. The Āshramas are exclusively brāhmans, and they predominate in the Tīrtha, the Bhāratī and the Saraswatī subsects.

The brahmachārīs, who are all brāhmans, were originally the pupils of the orders, as the name refers to the first stage of life, when the disciple

This graceful lady Sādhu, Sobhna Giri, belongs to the Junā Ākhārā. A young *Sādhvī* (female Sādhu) is a rare sight in the brotherhood of Sādhus, for unlike her, the few women who enter Sādhu-life, do so when they are much older, usually widowed or still unmarried.

lives with the teacher. But gradually the term acquired the meaning of 'celibate' and even 'lifelong celibate', as the brahmachārī renounced the second and third stages of life. Shankara is the prime example of the life-long celibate.

The viraktas are regarded as the purest renouncers, living the most simple life. Having given up their individuality they only move about in orderly groups. They keep silent most of the time, rarely speak with one another, and spend their time studying the scriptures and meditating.

Warrior Ascetics

A martial tradition has characterized Hindu asceticism from a very early period. There must have been individual yogīs and various groups of ascetics who bore arms since the prehistoric past, but they were hardly noticed until about the seventh century AD. These armed ascetics formed the nucleus around which the later warriors, who were recruited mainly from the lower castes, became organized. These are called Nāgā sannyāsīs, the 'naked renouncers', or in short Nāgās.

In response to the aggressive invasions of the Muslim armies who forcibly conquered and ruled much of India from 1200 AD, a vast increase in the number of militant ascetics occurred and they were organized into a system of 'regiments' called Ākhārās. Originally the meaning of ākhārā is 'a place to train the body, to have training in arms'. Obviously, these Ākhārās were not meant to be centres of religious learning, yet many of the Nāgās performed severe austerities and various yogic practices.

The Ākhārās attribute their origin to the great Shankara, an attempt no doubt to gain more respect and credibility, but in fact some were established much earlier, and some much later. Allowing for historical inaccuracy, the dates (AD) for the six Ākhārās are:[18]

Ānanda Ākhārā	856
Niranjanī Ākhārā	904
Junā Ākhārā	1106
Āvāhan Ākhārā	1547
Atal Ākhārā	1646
Nirvānī Ākhārā	1749

One more Ākhārā, properly not belonging to the dashnāmī sannyāsīs but nevertheless of Shaiva signature, is the Agni Ākhārā, which was

---

Opposite For centuries the Nāgā Bābās were the fearless ascetic warriors and it still shows in their display of weapons. Now, however, these are mostly magical 'weapons' and symbols of spiritual power. Mahant Darshan Giri's sash with medals – heroic symbols of the Nāgā's former enemies, the British – seems out of place, but it does add to his martial appearance.

Affiliated to the Junā Ākhārā is the subsect of Gudārs, which is distinguished by a curious form of ritualistic begging. In single file the Gudārs hurry through the Sādhu camps, the smallest Bābā trailing behind with a flag or a club. Holding out their coconut begging-bowls ('skulls') they shout 'Alakh!', invoking the Absolute, and stop for a moment at every Sādhu's fire to have their bowls filled with flour or rice. The leader of the group carries a bowl with burning incense and ashes, with which he marks the forehead of the Sādhus.

established in 1482 AD. The members of this Ākhārā are all brahmachārīs, the lifelong celibates mentioned above. They did not acquire equal status with the sannyāsī Ākhārās until 1971.

Originally there was not much difference between these Ākhārās. In the course of time however, they developed their own nuances in traditions and identities. For example, the Nirvānī wear their bundle of hair on the right, the Niranjanī in the middle and the Junā on the left.

There are also more important differences in discipline and rituals. One striking distinction of the Junā Ākhārā is the keeping of individual *dhūnīs*, or sacred fires. And on the whole the Nāgās of the Junā Ākhārā are more individualistic, less regimented; and they perform much more than the others the ancient ascetic rituals and practices, such as going about naked, wearing ashes, performing fire sacrifices, and so on. They have remained most faithful to the original image of the 'long-haired sage'.

Even though the official dates indicate otherwise, they regard themselves as the oldest Ākhārā, which is expressed in their name Junā Ākhārā, meaning 'old regiment'. Although they are a Shaiva sect, their present tutelary deity Dattātreya is a partial incarnation of the rival deity Vishnu, who nevertheless shows many Shaiva characteristics. He is a replacement

Dishāma Nāth, a Kānphatā Jogī, poses in front of a group of memorial stones at the cremation grounds on the beach in Dwarka. He wears the distinctive Gorakhnāthī necklace, with a small bone whistle as pendant, which he may blow to invoke his Guru and tutelary deity.

of their former tutelary deity Bhairava, who is depicted as always in ecstasy, surrounded by women, indulging in sex, drinking wine and eating flesh from a human skull. Since they shared a common tutelary deity, it seems logical to assume that the Nāgās were inspired by the Kāpālikas – who were also known as fighters – or even that they had common roots.

Dattātreya, as a manifestation of Bhairava, is regarded as a preceptor of non-Āryan tribes and can therefore be accompanied by four dogs,

Drinking out of a human skull is one of the striking peculiarities that differentiates the Aghorī from the average ascetic. It is a magical act: a partaking of the dead person's life-force. The skull contains the soul-spirit, as it has not been released by the proper rituals of cremation, which involve breaking the cranium. The Aghorī has control over this spirit by uttering the right *mantras* (here meaning magical incantations). He uses the genie as his 'slave', both in this world and the beyond: the skulls of this Aghorī dwelling in the cremation grounds (*above*) are on duty as his lookouts and lifeguard.

very inferior creatures but nevertheless representing the four Vedas. He is depicted as the three-faced mythological combination of the gods Brahmā, Shiva and Vishnu. Dattātreya, who also seems to have been a historical personage, is the only ascetic to have temples – as well as the Junā Ākhārā Nāgās – devoted to his worship.

The Kumbha Melās are very important events in the lives of Sādhus. In the past these Kumbha Melās, where all sects assemble every three years or so (see p. 103), were often the scene of fights and battles between Shaiva and Vaishnava Nāgās to determine the order of precedence in the bathing processions. This rivalry was not only based on religious and ideological differences or the determination of sectarian rank and status, for the Nāgās were also involved in warfare between rival princely states, usually fighting on opposite sides. Moreover, they fought for control of religious centres, since these constituted ever-flowing sources of revenue and solid bases of power. With the growth of British colonial domination in South Asia during the eighteenth and nineteenth centuries, however, martial asceticism was gradually suppressed.

Other Shaiva Sects

Besides these sannyāsīs, there are a few more major ascetic sects, the Gorakhnāthīs, the Aghorīs and the Udasīn.

The Gorakhnāthīs are commonly referred to as Yogīs or Jogīs. Although in outlook very similar to the sannyāsīs, the Jogīs do not follow the Vedantic teachings of Shankara, but adhere to the Tantric way taught by their Guru-founder Gorakhnāth. Still, they are devotees of Shiva, albeit in his manifestation as Bhairava, and they worship Hanumān and Dattātreya.

The myth of Gorakhnāth's divine descent clearly identifies the ancient sect of Kāpālikas as the origin of the Gorakhnāthīs. Gorakhnāth was one of twenty-four Kāpālikas who were made manifest by Shiva in order to fight against twenty-four incarnations of Vishnu. The Kāpālikas were victorious, chopped off the heads of Vishnu's incarnations, and henceforth carried these skulls in their hands. Gorakhnāth is worshipped as a deity by the Jogīs, and has a number of temples dedicated to him. The Jogīs are therefore often designated as 'Gorakhnāthīs', or more simply 'Nāth Bābās'.

One section of the Gorakhnāthīs goes by the name of Kānphatās – i.e. 'split ears' – which refers to their practice of piercing the central portion of the ears with the double-edged 'Bhairavi knife', and inserting large circular earrings during a second initiation. Before this rigorous operation the Nāth Bābās are called Aughārs, meaning 'unfinished',[19] and many will never reach the second stage. Aughārs should not be confused with Aghorīs, who constitute yet another section of the Gorakhnāthīs. And to complicate matters a little more, there are also Aghorīs who do not belong to the Gorakhnāthīs at all, as will be shown below.

In actual practice, thereby revealing their descent from the Kāpālikas, the ascetics of the Aghorī section of the Gorakhnāthīs still carry skulls; the other Bābās nowadays carry a coconut bowl, which however is still called *kapār*, that is, 'skull'.

There is not much difference between the Aghorīs of the Gorakhnāthīs, those belonging to the separate sect of Aghorīs, and those individual 'independent' practitioners who do not belong to any sect. More than any other group of ascetics, they can be seen as the direct descendants of the Kāpālikas. In outlook and practices they must resemble Bhairavāchārya (see p. 17), and like him worship Shiva in one of his ferocious manifestations.

The Aghorīs stand closest to the ancient shamanistic ascetics, who by incantations and witchcraft sought to control ghosts and spirits; and they stand furthest from respectable society, since they transgress all the rules. They drink alcohol, eat meat – even human flesh, it is said – and abuse people with foul and obscene language. The gruesome practice of human sacrifices has disappeared (perhaps not totally – they can be quite 'conservative' in these matters) and the eating of human flesh is certainly not a daily occurrence. So in all probability their 'cannibalism' is nowadays merely symbolic.

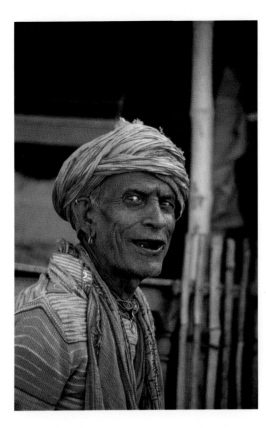

There is a metaphysical logic behind this deviant behaviour that defines the Aghorīs as real ascetics and not just 'degraded' madmen. They aspire to a state of enlightenment in which there is no differentiation between opposites and no distinction between the soul and the Absolute. The Aghorī way of dissolving this metaphysical duality is to insist unconditionally on the common identity of mundane opposites – bad is good, death is life, dirty is clean, etc. – and to act this out concretely.

The Aghorīs' distinctly provocative behaviour is another characteristic they have in common with the shamans, who 'communicated' by obscene and abusive language, incoherent talk, animal noises, and crying for no apparent reason. This was – and is – regarded as proof of supernatural abilities. In this respect they are not much different from other Bābās, who may occasionally exhibit similar symptoms of 'divine madness'.

The total number of Aghorī ascetics is very small, and even fewer are the real radicals. The way of the Aghorī is certainly not a popular form of asceticism. Courting and suffering disrespect must be the hardest part. For respect is the one earthly reward that most Bābās still cherish – and, mostly, deserve.

The Udasīn were originally not Shaiva, nor even Hindu, but belonged to the Sikh religion. The sect was founded in the sixteenth century by a son of Guru Nānak – himself the founder of Sikhism – called Shrīchandra. The Udasīn are therefore also known as Nānakputras, the 'sons of Nānak', and they revere the Granth Saheb, the sacred book of the Sikhs. They were excommunicated by the successor of Guru Nānak and gradually turned instead to Hinduism.

Mishri Dās has joined the Udasīn at a very early age, which is not unusual. Boy-Bābās are treated with a mixture of respect and endearment; they are given some general education and preliminary ascetic instructions. But they will only be fully initiated when they are older and fully aware of the consequences of this momentous decision.

The Udasīn worship a combination of five deities, namely Shiva, Vishnu, the Sun, goddess Durgā, and the son of Shiva, Ganesh; moreover, they worship their founder, Guru Shrīchandra. Their philosophy is basically the monistic Vedānta as set forth by Shankara, and in other respects as well they closely resemble the Shaiva sannyāsīs. Furthermore, whenever in the past they had to choose sides in fights with rival sects, they took the part of the Shaivas.

Nirvāna Rāma Dās (*left*) and Ananda Rāma Dās, two Udasīn Bābās. Upon initiation
into the sect, the novitiate is given a new name with the suffix *Dās* ('slave' or
'servant') or *Muni* ('sage'). These suffixes do not imply any rank or status and
are apparently given at random. The principal part of the initiation consists of
the 'drinking of *amrit*' (the nectar of immortality), which is water consecrated
by letting it flow over the feet of the Guru, to which a little sugar is added.

3 Vishnu

The world of Vishnu contrasts with Shiva's as day and night. At the same time they form a complementary whole, the Yin and Yang of Hinduism, to borrow a foreign concept: Shiva is the moon god, the aloof ascetic, alone in the heart of the infinite; Vishnu the sun god, the merciful warrior king, the close friend of mankind who descends to earth whenever the world has to be saved from doom. In the pantheon Vishnu resides at the same level as Shiva, alongside Brahmā in the divine trinity. Self-evidently, in the hearts of his devotees he is the Supreme Lord, the one and only.

The Pervader

Vishnu's body is blue, the colour of the sky, for he is the 'Pervader', who in a mythological contest won the three regions of the universe by striding across it in three steps. Metaphysically the Pervader need not have done so, for his essence is of course everywhere simultaneously, connecting all.

As an omnipotent Hindu god, Vishnu has four arms. He holds three weapons and a lotus. His unique weapon is a revolving missile, the flaming sun-wheel circling around his right index finger. It is called *su-darshan*, 'beautiful vision', and symbolizes the unlimited expanse and speed of his mind. It represents the cycle of the sun, and the cycle of creation, preservation and destruction, effortlessly kept in motion by Lord Vishnu. As a weapon – much like Shiva's trident – the discus is used to combat evil and ignorance. Vishnu's second weapon is the mace, representing kinetic energy at rest, a symbol of authority like the royal sceptre. His third attribute, the conch shell, or *shankh*, can be interpreted as a weapon, since one of its original uses was as a horn in war. It produces a piercing sound, a far-reaching call for battle, though in Vishnu's hand it is primarily a symbol of generation. The white conch, with its smooth, rounded contours and soft pink interior, evidently resembles the vulva,

---

Opposite The Sītā-Rāma Bābās, as Vaishnavas are popularly called, are easily recognized by the white or yellow clothes they usually wear and the vertical tilak painted on the forehead.

the divine womb out of which the five elements are born: earth, water, fire, air and ether. When the shankh is blown by Vishnu, it produces the primal sound – like Shiva's rattling damaru – the tone of Creation.

The Creator

In his lower left hand Vishnu holds a budding white and red lotus. The lotus, or *padma*, must be the most ubiquitous symbol in Hinduism, and is generally considered to represent the spiritual evolution of man, his ultimate perfection and purity: the transformation of muddy matter into life, a plant that rises through the dark and turbulent water-world, with its flowers unfolding in the open air to shine in the sun, their beauty unsoiled by mud or water. This metaphor also explains the origin of the word *padmāsana* to denote the yogic posture par excellence, the 'lotus posture': the lower part of the body is in the mud, the middle part in the water, and the upper part of the skull sticks out of the water, where the consciousness, the 'thousand-petalled lotus' can unfold, to be enlightened by the sun.

The lotus is also a sexual symbol. After all, the flower is the generative organ of the plant. The lotus, with its silky, fleshy petals curving around the tender interior that exudes fragrant pollen, has inspired many poetical comparisons to the vulva. *'Om! mani padme hum'*, the well-known Tantric mantra meaning 'Om! jewel in the lotus', obviously intimates that the linga is in the yoni. It is no accident that the padmāsana is the favourite posture of the gods making love, fusing the opposites, performing the yab-yum of creation, to borrow a Tibetan concept.

The Lotus Goddess

Vishnu's divine consort, or female counterpart, is the lotus goddess Padmā, better known as Shrī, the resplendent Earth-mother, or as Lakshmī. She emerged from the milky ocean when it was churned at the dawn of creation, and is seated on a giant lotus, floating on the surface, surrounded by many small lotuses of different colours, with honey bees buzzing around. In her upper right hand she holds a thousand-petalled lotus, in her upper left hand a hundred-petalled lotus and on her head she wears a lotus crown.

Out of her lower left hand flows a steady stream of gold coins, for she is the goddess of Plenty. She bestows prosperity on all her devotees: not merely material wealth, but also physical wellbeing, mental brightness and spiritual enlightenment. She is the archetypal *padminī*, the 'lotus woman', the eternal ideal of feminine beauty, loveliness and grace.

Vishnu, of Āryan descent, was only a minor solar deity in early Vedic times. Ascending the steps of the pantheon, moving to centre-stage, he took over the roles of various existing gods, primarily the part of Indra, the former chief deity. He rose to eminence mainly on the popularity of his two human incarnations, king Rāma and cowherd Krishna. He had

Mahant Bhagawān Dās raises his hand in blessing. Iconographically this hand-position (*mudrā*) is known as the *abhaya-mudrā*, expressing 'have no fear'. He was a *khareshwarī* ('standing' Bābā) for twenty-eight years, but had to end this austerity several years ago, on doctor's orders.

जय श्री राम

Jay Shrī Rāma

Followers of Rāma with very
distinct sectarian marks.
Within a sect the tilaks are
seldom entirely identical. Most
Bābās give them a personal
touch, but some make more
extreme variations on the basic
theme. The result can be quite
impressive, as is shown by
Hanumān Hari Dās (*opposite*)
and Rāma Chandra Dās (*right*)
but it does not necessarily imply
a higher status. Nor does it, by
itself, reflect a higher degree of
spirituality. A distinctive feature
of some Shrī Mahants is a
'crown' of jatā, as worn here by
Rāma Krishan Dās (*below right*),
and adorned with tiger claws to
increase its projection of power.

incarnated before, in various animal avatāras and as a dwarf, in effect going through evolutionary stages; he incarnated as the Buddha, and will incarnate once more as Kalkī, the Saviour.

Rāma and Sītā

Rāma, the seventh avatāra of Vishnu, and his wife Sītā, are the hero and heroine of the Ramayana, the 'Life of Rāma', the grand epic poem composed between the fifth century BC and second century AD. However, when people refer to the Ramayana, they usually mean the sixteenth-century vernacular version composed by the poet–saint Tulsīdās. For devotees of Rāma it is the bible.

The Ramayana can be understood on many levels. On a mundane level it details the Āryan subjugation of the indigenous tribes in the south and the just rule of an enlightened king who instituted a legendary golden age. The villain of the story is Rāvana, the king of Lankā and leader of the indigenous tribes, who is portrayed as the ten-headed, twenty-armed demon-leader of a black-faced sub-human race.

The plot of Rāma's divine drama centres around his union with Sītā and their temporary separation. Rāma, the rightful heir to the throne of Ayodhya, is exiled from the kingdom for fourteen years. Accompanied by his wife and his faithful half-brother Lakshmana, he retires to the jungle near Chitrakut, where they lead a life of renunciation and asceticism. One day Sītā is abducted by the demon-king Rāvana, disguised as a holy man, who flies off with her to Lankā, his island-city of gold, where he imprisons her on top of a mountain.

Rāma and Lakshmana assemble an army of monkeys and bears, an expeditionary force for rescuing Sītā. A supporting role is played by Rāma's trusted lieutenant Hanumān, the general of the monkeys, who is half-man, half-ape. But he is divine too, through his deep devotion for the Lord.

Naturally, the Hero and the Villain have to meet face to face. Rāma's arrows, swift as lightning, cut off Rāvana's ten heads. Evil is conquered, liberated by Rāma's grace, and transformed to Good. Sītā and Rāma are re-united and they return triumphantly to heavenly Ayodhya, where Rāma assumes his rightful place on the throne. On this level the Ramayana is an allegory of the soul's separation from, and eventual merging with the Absolute.

As mythology, Rāma's adventures and tribulations are regarded as his divine 'play', in which he shows humanity the path of salvation through exclusive devotion to him. The unswerving adoration of Rāma's companions and attendants sets an example for all mortals who want to experience his presence or receive his grace. The ultimate message of the Ramayana is therefore that surrender and devotion to Rāma conquers the evil in oneself, and removes the obstacles on the path to liberation and enlightenment.

Shrī Mahant Sunmarpan Dās, as his title indicates (Shrī referring to the resplendent Goddess) has a high position in the Vaishnava religious hierarchy. As prescribed in the holy scriptures, he has also painted tilaks on other parts of the body: the basic 'U' design on his upper arms and a *chakra*, the whirling sun-disc of Vishnu, on the shoulders.

The Rāmāyana was made into a television series, which ran for several years. It was immensely popular, even if it contained much dialogue and little action. When it was broadcast each Sunday morning, the streets of India were empty: groups of ten to thirty people watched the neighbourhood television set. Sādhus watched as well, and not only devotees of Rāma. In the Rāmāyana extensive homage is paid to Shiva

– in fact he is the narrator of the story – and he in his turn worships Rāma. On this divine level Rāma is the all-Hindu deity.

Krishna and Rādhā

Vishnu's eighth incarnation is Krishna, the Dark Lord, the young boy-prince and romantic cowherd. His heroic and amorous exploits – and their divine nature – are described in the Mahābhārata, the Purānas (collections of ancient legends and mythologies) and in numerous lyrical hymns and love-poems.

The Mahābhārata, composed between 500 BC and AD 400, is, like the Rāmāyana, on a mundane level the legend of a war, which supposedly took place in 1400 BC. Two families descended from the mythical king Bhārata, the Pāndavas and the Kauravas, fight over the possession of a kingdom that is also called 'Bhārata'; hence the title of the tragedy, 'Great (Story of) Bhārata'.

The life of Krishna in particular is described in a later addition to the Mahābhārata, and his role in the war is elucidated in the Bhagavad Gītā, the 'Song of the Lord', an integral part of the epic. The Bhagavad Gītā is the dialogue between Krishna and Arjuna, the Pāndava prince and hero, taking place during their eighteen days on the battlefield. Arjuna the reluctant warrior would rather give up his own life than kill his fellow men; and Krishna, his charioteer must remind him of his duty and enlighten him about the facts of life and death.[20]

> As a man, casting off worn-out garments, taketh new ones, so the dweller in the body, casting off worn-out bodies, entereth into others that are new.
>
> Further, looking to thine own duty, thou shouldst not tremble; for there is nothing more welcome to a warrior than righteous war.
>
> Taking as equal pleasure and pain, gain and loss, victory and defeat, gird thee for the battle; thus thou shalt not incur sin.

Thus the Bhagavad Gītā teaches the metaphysical truths about the soul, rebirth and karma ('fate'). It teaches not the renunciation of action, but rather renouncing the fruits of action. More important still, Krishna stresses that devotion to him, bhakti, is the only way to reach liberation. It seems easier, however, to love him in his other role, as the younger Krishna, the naughty boy – though a slayer of demons as well – the enchanting cowherd playing his magic flute, 'dallying' with his beloved Rādhā and his adorable gopīs, the girls tending the cows in the woods of Brindavan.

His affair with Rādhā may have been illicit, since in some accounts she is the wife of another cowherd, but it does not really matter whether

Krishna Govinda, the divine cowherd, playing his magic flute in the pastoral setting of Brindavan.

she was married. After all, Krishna is a god whose aims are by definition inscrutable, and on a divine level Rādhā is Lakshmī and Shrī, the lotus goddess and beloved of Vishnu.

Again, as in the Rāmāyana, the main theme is love and attraction, separation and reunion. Similarly this love affair should be understood as a metaphor of the soul's yearning for union with the Absolute. Nevertheless, the numerous songs and poems devoted to Rādhā–Krishna's sacred love are filled with earthly erotic imagery. The most renowned of them is the 'Song of the Divine Cowherd', the Gītāgovinda, composed by the twelfth-century poet Jayadeva.[21]

> As he rests in Shrī's embrace,
> On the soft slope of her breast,
> The saffroned chest of the demon's killer
> Is stained with red marks of passion
> And sweat from fatigue of tumultuous longing.
> May his broad chest bring you pleasure too!

Krishna, also called Hari, an epithet of Vishnu, certainly brings pleasure to the other girls of Brindavan. They dance in circles on the banks of the Yamuna, each gopī imagining that she is the only one loved, but Krishna is multi-form and enjoys them all simultaneously.

> He hugs one, he kisses another, he caresses another dark beauty,
> He stares at one's suggestive smiles, he mimics a wilful girl.
> Hari revels here as the crowd of charming girls
> revels in seducing him to play.

Deserted and in anguish, Rādhā uses all her charm and wit to win him back, asking one of the girls to act as a go-between, as a sakhī, to bring messages of love – and pain. Finally she succeeds, Krishna gives up the other girls and now longs only for her. One night they meet again.

> *Displaying her passion*
> *In loveplay as the battle began,*
> *She launched a bold offensive*
> *Above him*
> *And triumphed over her lover.*
> *Her hips were still,*
> *Her vine-like arm was slack,*
> *Her chest was heaving,*
> *Her eyes were closed.*
> *Why does a mood of manly force*
> *Succeed for women in love?*

Again, only love will do: surrender and devotion. Yet the bhakti of the Gītāgovinda – sacred but sexual passion – is a world apart from the unattached devotion of the Bhagavad Gītā, even though they are both directed at the same deity, Krishna.

The type of ecstatic devotion engendered by the Gītāgovinda became the basic feature of a number of bhakti cults. The devotees would identify themselves with Rādhā; just as she longs for her lover, they would yearn for Krishna. Moreover, they held the view – as implied in the Gītāgovinda – that carnal love was basically identical to spiritual love. In the early days this was taken quite literally as the 'left-handed way', but in contemporary bhakti cults it is replaced by the 'right-handed way', the contemplative imagination of erotic fusion with Krishna, or, better, the passionate longing to witness Rādhā and Krishna fusing.

Surrender and Devotion

Possibly the most influential reformer of Vaishnavism was Rāmānuja, respectfully known as Rāmānujāchārya, 'teacher Rāmānuja', who lived in the twelfth century. He wrote extensive philosophical commentaries on the Vedānta, established numerous temples and converted many people to Vaishnavism, most of whom were householders, not ascetics. He founded the earliest of the traditional Vaishnava sects, the Shrī Sampradāya, also known as the Rāmānujīs.

Opposite A cold morning in Hardwar on the banks of the holy Ganges. Hanumān Dās and his Sādhu-brother have spent the night here and are now engrossed in their morning rituals. Hanumān Dās is painting his tilak, while in the background a Jangam musician – whose ancestors were renegade Shaiva Sādhus – sings his devotional songs.

Rāmānuja strongly opposed Shankara's monism, calling him a 'crypto-Buddhist' whose conception of the Brahman was too similar to the Buddhist 'void' (*shūnya*). Instead he propounded what is known as 'qualified monism'. Metaphysically this can be described as the identification of the immanent Absolute with a transcendental, personal god, who creates or destroys the world as part of his divine 'play'. The Brahman, though One, may manifest himself in various forms, and may descend on earth in animal or human form in order to protect the good, punish the wicked and restore the Law.

The individual soul is an attribute or mode of Brahman and forms part of his 'body', yet is simultaneously a spiritual substance in itself and absolutely real. It is beyond creation and destruction; it is an eternal point of spiritual light. At birth it is embodied according to its karma; after death, if it is still tinged with karma, it has to descend to the world again. Through liberation the soul is cleansed of karma and needs no further reincarnation. Brahman is the master of the Law of Karma, and is the inner controller of the soul – yet, paradoxically, the soul has freedom of will.

So karma has to be removed through right action, and ignorance through real knowledge, for liberation to take place. Right action is the performance of one's duties, as laid down in the Vedas, in an absolutely disinterested manner. These are not merely 'good deeds', as is demonstrated by Arjuna, who in performing his duty as a warrior has to kill his brothers.

> He that performeth such action as is duty,
> independently of the fruit of action,
> he is an ascetic, he is a Yogī,
> not that he is without fire and without rites.[22]

Real knowledge is not just discursive knowledge of the scriptures – which is nevertheless indispensable – but is identified with the highest bhakti or devotion, which consists of self-surrender to the Brahman and constant remembrance of him. The immediate intuitive knowledge of him, however, may only be gained through his divine grace (*prasād*). The liberated soul does not become identical with Brahman, but only similar to him, enjoying in direct communion infinite consciousness and infinite bliss.

As an integral part of his philosophy Rāmānuja replaced the impersonal, abstract Brahman with the more 'human' Vishnu as a personal

---

Opposite This Bābā carrying a yoke is a member of a small and elusive group of Rāmānandās. Individually these ascetics make their daily rounds from Sādhu to Sādhu, detached and self-effacing, silently collecting foodstuffs – mainly flour and rice – for the subsequent preparation of free meals for poor Bābās and pilgrims.

Mathurā Dās belongs to the tyāgī (renouncer) subsect of the Rāmānandā Sādhus
who follow very strict ascetic rules. He started Sādhu-life at the age of seven, when
he was adopted by an old Bābā after his parents drowned in the Ganges at the 1953
Kumbha Melā in Hardwar, where a bridge collapsed under the weight of pilgrims.
Divine providence.

god. For the Brahman of the Vedānta cannot really be loved. Love presupposes duality – the lover and the beloved – and Brahman and the soul are one, so quite logically pure monism precludes love.

The Four Sects

In the centuries following Rāmānuja, three more Vaishnava sects were founded, by Nimbārka, Madhva and Vallabha: the Sanaka Sampradāya more popularly known as Nimbārkīs; the Brahmā Sampradāya or Mādhvīs; and the Rudra Sampradāya or Vallabhīs.

Each of these teachers expounded his own theological system, essentially based on Rāmānuja's qualified monism, with some amendments and modifications, and hence with new labels such as 'qualified dualism' and 'unqualified dualism'.

They advocated the worship of a different deity, though still an avatāra of Vishnu, substituting Krishna and his consort Rādhā in place of Vishnu and Lakshmī. Consequently the concept of bhakti underwent an important change. It was no longer 'knowledge' of Vishnu, but a much more emotional, at times even sentimental, all-surpassing love and affection for Krishna.

A very successful ascetic sect was founded by Rāmānanda, also known as Rāmānandāchārya near the beginning of the fourteenth century: the Rāmānanda Sampradāya, more popularly called the Rāmānandīs. Nowadays, because of its dominant position, it is regarded as a separate organization, but officially it is still part of the Shrī Sampradāya, for Rāmānanda started his ascetic career as a member of this sect. He remained loyal to the philosophy of its founder Rāmānuja, but he did replace Vishnu and Lakshmī with Rāma and Sītā as personal gods, and made devotion to them the central feature of the sect's religious practices.

Rāmānanda spent most of his life in Benares, which was for many centuries the holy city of Shaiva ascetics and has become the unofficial centre of all ascetics. He lived at a time when Islam was rapidly spreading across India, and made it his duty to defend Hinduism by political activism. Since the lower castes and *pariahs* especially were converted to Islam, it may have been for opportunistic reasons that he opened his sect to members of all castes, women and even Muslims, but equally he may have been genuinely egalitarian. Certainly, his 'caste-no-bar' policy did not survive long after his death.

The last major Vaishnava sect, affiliated to the Brahmā Sampradāya, is the Gaurīya Sampradāya. It was founded by the sixteenth-century saint Chaitanya, who was believed to be an incarnation of Krishna, or rather Rādhā–Krishna. His followers dedicated a number of temples to him and worship him as their tutelary deity.

With him the 'right-handed' bhakti cult reached a new height and a certain respectability. He was a very emotional ascetic, bhakti incarnate, and showered love and affection on those around him. In long-lasting ecstatic trances he lost all consciousness of the external world and had to be taken care of as a child. In certain periods, when he fused completely with the personality of Rādhā, he used to wear women's clothes.

Dispassion

The traditional framework of Vaishnava sectarianism thus consists of four major sects representing related, more or less competing, philosophical and religious positions. Of these only the Nimbārkīs and Rāmānandīs have appreciable numbers of ascetics, and in practice the Rāmānanda Sampradāya is so large that it virtually constitutes Vaishnava asceticism.

Vaishnava ascetics are called *bairāgīs*, which literally means 'detached' or 'dispassionate'. Nevertheless, they are not so detached as to have abolished caste distinctions, though efforts have been made. As with the Shaivas, only brāhmans are allowed to carry a stick, the danda, as a symbol of authority. Differing from the Shaiva danda, this stick consists of three bamboo sticks bound together.

Within the Rāmānandī sect, a distinct group of bairāgīs who have undergone further initiation confirming their vow to adhere to more severe rules of asceticism, are titled *tyāgīs*, that is 'renouncers', and *mahā-tyāgīs*, 'great renouncers'; the latter, as their title implies, are even more austere. The initiation is known as *khāk-dīkshā*, or 'ash-initiation', after which the tyāgī is privileged – and obliged – to wear ashes. Tyāgīs subject themselves to various forms of austerities, such as hatha yoga, continuous exposure to the elements and *dhūnī-tap*, (fire-austerities, see pp. 156 and 161).

A further distinction is made between those ascetics who semi-permanently reside in monasteries, the *sthānādhārīs*; those who belong to wandering groups, the *khālsās*; and those who form the 'fighting' detachments, the *ākhārāmallas*. The sthānādhārīs and khālsās form the regular ascetic sections, distinct from the militant ākhārāmallas.

Fighting Ascetics

The regiments of militant bairāgīs closely resemble the Ākhārā organizations of the Shaiva militants, the Nāgās, and are therefore often designated as 'Nāgās' as well. This may be confusing, since bairāgīs are never naked and nakedness is specifically associated with the term Nāgā. In fact, they, or some of them at least, might have been naked in former times, since the name of the oldest and most important regiment is Digambar, usually translated as 'sky-clad', thus naked. In Vaishnava circles however it is, nowadays at least, interpreted as 'the four directions', thus omnipresence or boundlessness or similar lofty concepts.

The first Vaishnava Ākhārās were organized in the seventeenth century – much later than the Shaiva Ākhārās – out of formerly separate groups of fighting ascetics of various sects. As the most militant, the Rāmānandī sect played a leading role in the formation of the Ākhārās;

their Digambar Ākhārā enjoys 'the privilege of being the custodian of the foot-prints of Rāmānanda', which 'by itself confirms its pristine antiquity'.[23]

The original seven Ākhārās – Digambar, Nirvānī, Nirmohī, Khākī, Niralambī, Santoshī and Mahānirvānī – were further organized in three *anīs*, or 'divisions': the Digambar, Nirmohī and Nirvānī. Again there is potential confusion, since the anīs have the same names as three Ākhārās, but usually these Ākhārās are further distinguished by adding a qualifying term based on the name of the founder or the tutelary deity.

At the Kumbha Melā each anī camps separately from the others, displaying its distinctive regimental banners. These huge triangular flags are

Mahant Gyān Dās is the head of the subsect of Rāmānandī Wrestlers. Their tutelary deity is Hanumān, the monkey god, the most loyal servant of Lord Rāma and general of the monkey army. The worship of Hanumān is widespread and usually not different from the worship of other deities. The Wrestlers, however, stress one particular aspect, his fighting spirit.

Umesh Dās sits in the sand-filled arena where the Wrestlers exercise and hold their sparring matches. The sand is sacred and may intentionally be rubbed on face and body as a sign of devotion – and exertion.

Opposite Rāmānandāchārya Rāmeshwarānanda, one of the four contemporary successors of Rāmānanda, carries the *tri-danda* as evidence of his religious authority. Consisting of three bamboo sticks tightly bound together, the tri-danda symbolizes the three interconnected aspects of asceticism: control of body, speech and mind. It is rarely carried, for with the tri-danda in the hand, one cannot bow for anyone, including superiors, and this would certainly be interpreted as arrogance.

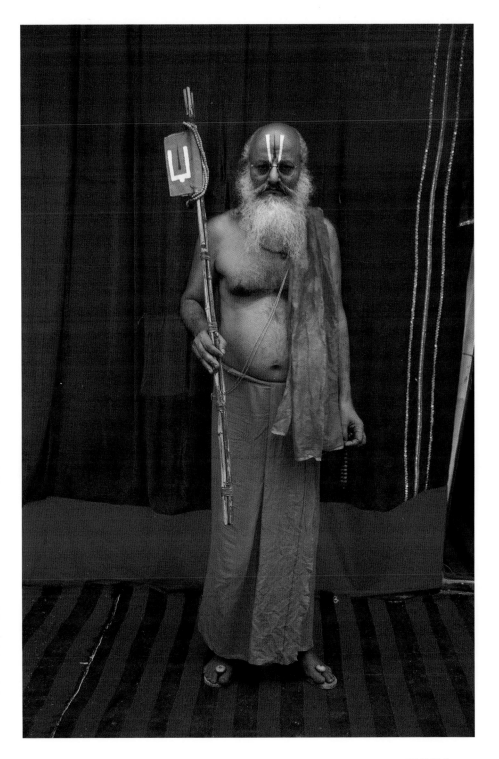

made from the finest silk and embroidered with gold and silver thread. The cloth is attached to a long pole, which has two spearheads on each end, and is also called *anī*, meaning 'spear'. Needless to say, these anīs are treated with the utmost reverence. With colours flying, the Bābās carry the flags in the festive bathing processions, taking them for a bath as well: the two spearheads of each are ceremonially dipped into the water.

Subsects

The many Vaishnava subsects are virtually autonomous; the Mahant ('great leader') of even the smallest āshram is in fact his own boss. He is the much-revered Guru, who governs undisputedly, very individually,

Rāma Brahmadeo Sharan (*above*) and Janaki Jivan Sharan (*opposite*) follow the rasik tradition, which emphasizes devotion to and refuge (*sharan*) in the female consort of the deity. As 'companions' of the goddess, they ritually enact a female role, for traditionally she can only be served by women. In sharp contrast with Sakhīs, the 'sharans' do not outwardly show the feminine attitude underlying their devotional practices, but 'live' it. Their aim is mystical union through inner – not outer – transformation.

Jhunjhunia Bābā, so nicknamed because of the ankle-bells he used to wear as a young Sakhī, does not care much about appearances any more. He is beyond that now.

but as a rule respecting the traditions established by the preceptors in his line. This allows for a great variety of ascetic lifestyles among sects, symbolically expressed by variations in dress, hair, forehead marks, rituals and tutelary deities. Within a sect, however, the code is uniform.

Some sects have age-old traditions that set them strikingly apart from the mainstream. For instance, the much respected Rāmānandī subsect of Wrestlers. In girth sometimes approaching the Japanese sumo wrestlers, they devote a large part of their daily life to body-building in honour of Lord Hanumān, their tutelary deity. Since there are no longer any real opportunities to prove their wrestling prowess in combat, this should be regarded as devotional, bodily emulation of Hanumān.

A totally different section of the Rāmānandīs is formed by the *rasik* branch, who show the strong influence of 'right-handed' shākta cults and do not repress their erotic longings – as ascetics are wont to do – but focus them on the deity of their choice. Rasik is derived from the word *rasa*, a concept with many related meanings, which in the first instance can be translated as 'juice', 'elixir', 'essence' and 'taste'. On another level rasa means 'pleasure', particularly the 'pleasures of love', and moreover the biological 'essences' of love: the 'love-juice' and 'love-seed'. As exemplified by Krishna, who is amorous love incarnate, the embodiment of rasa, it is the supreme joy of union with the divine. Rasa is the blissful essence of all.

The vast majority of Vaishnavas adopt the most suitable role of 'servant' as their 'personal relation' with the deity, which they express by adding the suffix 'Dās', that is 'slave' or 'servant', to their name. The rasiks by contrast emulate either the role of female companion of Sītā or Rādhā, or the role of 'mistress' of Rāma or Krishna.

The rasiks are consequently characterized by a certain femininity. The rasik as unselfish 'companion', does not strive for his own union with the divine; he would be overjoyed just to witness the eternal love-play of the deities.

On the other hand, the rasik sect of Sakhīs consists of male transvestites, who very concretely embody the role of 'mistress'. They shape their passionate longing for union with Rāma or Krishna on the sexual 'plays' of the deities as these are exemplified in the scriptures. The Sakhīs may envision themselves as one of the gopīs, particularly the 'love-messenger' (*sakhī*) between Rādhā and Krishna; or more exclusively, perhaps arrogantly, as his mistress Rādhā, or even – almost blasphemously – as Rāma's wife Sītā. Needless to say, the Sakhīs are viewed with some suspicion and derision, for sublimation of sexuality is the respected way, not its carnal projection.

Sakhīs, the rather obscure and controversial religious transvestites, not only dress like women, they also affect exaggerated feminine mannerisms. Moreover, it is rumoured that Sakhīs pretend to have carnal intercourse with the Lord at night – ecstatic cries and all – except when they have their 'period' and are impure for three days. Premalātha Sakhī (*above*) has dressed herself up in her finest sari and trinkets. It is Rāma's birthday (Rāma-nomī) and she will dance for her Lord in the temple.

4 The Life

No doubt the main motivating factor for joining the brotherhood of Sādhus is the desire for spiritual enlightenment, which is still strongly felt in India, where life is inextricably intertwined with religion, and where frequent encounters with holy men, who promise fulfilment of that desire, are part of growing up. But other, more mundane factors also play a role.

Asceticism, especially in its 'romantic' aspect of the powerful shaman or medicine man, can be regarded as an attractive option for the more adventurous, a challenging alternative sanctioned by ancient traditions. Another traditional aspect of the Sādhu – that of the philosopher–saint – may explain the attraction of an ascetic career for young students of Indian philosophy, the promise of a carefree life devoted to study.

For members of the lower castes who rebel against the confines of their status, becoming a holy man is one of the few ways to transcend it: to gain respect and to lead a comparatively free life. Some independent-minded youths rebel against the shackles of family life and marital obligations. The respectable way out is asceticism, renouncing the family and its worries. These adventurers and rebels, boys in their puberty or early adolescence, run away from home and start looking for a Guru.

The decision of older men, already weary of worldly life, to join a sect is often caused by traumatic events, such as the death of a family member, the loss of property or job, or an almost fatal accident. These are seen as a divine signal, the hand of God. Or they may just follow the ancient injunction to devote the fourth stage of life to renunciation and contemplation.

There is an old and persistent rumour that Sādhus steal children to turn them into disciples, but there is no hard evidence to support this accusation. The rumour is kept alive by parents who use the Sādhus as bogeymen, warning their children that if they do not behave properly, a Bābā will take them away in his Sādhu-bag.

Opposite Parashurāma Bhāratī in holy Hardwar, where the mighty Ganges flows into the plains. He has left the body now: he has 'gone to Kailash', the mountain-abode of Shiva, high in the Himalayas.

Sādhus do, however, take in foundlings and orphans, while some parents will give their son to a Sādhu as part of a 'deal' they have made with a deity for receiving some boon; or when the child shows certain symptoms (astrological, physical, mental) of predestination for spiritual life.

Asceticism is predominantly a male affair. Less than ten per cent of all Sādhus are female and most of them are widows. Traditionally, widows occupy a very marginal position in Hindu society, a remnant of the ancient belief that a woman does not deserve to live after her husband's death and should in fact have immolated herself on her husband's funeral pyre.

Quite a few sects do not allow women because of their 'corrupting influences'; some sects are mixed, but the female Sādhus, called Sādhvīs, usually have their separate quarters; and some minor subsects are all-female. There have been great female saints, but generally speaking their position in the spiritual hierarchy is inferior to men. On the personal level of Sādhu to Sādhvī, the women are treated with respect, but the popular belief is that Sādhvīs have to be born again as men before they can be liberated.

Many Sādhus today possess 'luxury' items by ascetic standards, such as watches, transistor radios and cassette recorders; and they use modern conveniences including electricity, telephones and public transport. However, their basic lifestyle has retained many archaic characteristics from the Stone and Bronze Ages. As a result, joining the brotherhood of Sādhus is like going back in time, being reborn in a semi-nomadic 'tribe' of the pre-agrarian age. It reflects a nostalgia for humanity's roots, for the simple, harmonious existence; alternatively, it might also be called an escape from the misery, pressures and complexities of this age.

Rebirth

The tribulations of the search for the right Guru form a recurring theme in folk tales and legends, along with his acceptance of the disciple, usually involving some kind of ordeal. In real life it is not much different. But there are Gurus who would accept almost anyone, since having disciples increases one's status, possibly one's income and certainly one's leisure. Starting as a disciple (chelā) with the Guru should mean behaving like his obliging son, but often entails working as an obedient servant, almost like a slave. If the apprentice is deemed fit for the ascetic life, he will receive preliminary instructions and be prepared for the initiation.

There are quite a few differences in initiations between sects, but they all centre around the symbolism of rebirth. At the moment of initiation the chelā severs all ties with family, clan or caste. He 'dies' from his former earthly life and is 'reborn' into the divine life. Any talk or thought about the former life is discouraged; it is irrelevant now and age is reckoned from the new birthday. The visible symbol of this rebirth is the shaven head, bald as a baby's. Shaivas shave all hair off, but the Vaishnavas leave

Tyāgī Bābā is the caretaker of this mud temple on Omkareshwar, the holy 'OM'-shaped island in the Narmada River. Pilgrims making the tour around the island will have *darshan* of Hanumān – the red-painted relief – and of the Bābā. In exchange they will deposit some coins for the upkeep of the shrine and the Bābā. A boy from the village ceremonially pours Narmada water over Hanumān.

Overleaf The initiation ceremonies of the Junā Ākhārā on the bank of the Shipra River during the Kumbha Melā at Ujjain. About 3,000 new disciples took part just for this Ākhārā – impressive evidence of the attraction Sādhu-life still has.

a small tuft of hair, the *shikhā*. The chelā receives a new name from his Guru, resounding with religious meaning, befitting his character, and indicative of his sectarian affiliation and preceptorial line.

The best time and place for initiation is at the Kumbha Melā (see pp. 141–46). For some sects, such as the Nāgās, this is the only occasion. Three days before the main bath, the novice's head is shaved, but the shikhā remains. He removes his old clothes and puts on a new white loincloth. He selects a twig from a special tree, which represents his staff, or danda, and fasts for the next three days, chanting mantras. Then, with his group of fellow initiates, he undergoes the funerary ceremony on the bank of the sacred river. Now he has died. He leaves his danda, renounces it, and his shikhā is shorn off by his Guru. Together they all take their bath, rub their bodies with ashes and return to their camp, where they receive their personal mantra from the Guru.

The Brotherhood

The bond with the Guru is now all-important. He is the 'dispeller of darkness', the guide who will lead him towards the Absolute. The chelā serves and worships the Guru as god-incarnate; he will please him any way he can. The Guru for his part takes full responsibility for the disciple's life; he has taken on the chelā's bad karma, he will feed him, instruct him, guide him. He will be more than his father. At least that is the ideal, and it exists. But there are a lot of chelās who grumble about their Guru, behind his back of course: they have to work too hard, he does not teach them the powerful mantras, he is not kind enough, and so on. Similarly, some Gurus complain about their chelās: they are lazy, disobedient, stupid, not like the chelās of the good old days, as they were themselves.

After initiation, the brotherhood of Sādhus more or less replaces the chelā's former family, as shown by the terms used to describe the relations between its members. The other disciples of one's Guru are called *guru-bhāī*, that is 'guru-brother', the Guru's Guru is called *dādā-guru*, meaning 'grandfather-guru', and so on. The relationship between guru-bhāīs is almost as important as the one with the Guru, and is usually very close and affectionate.

Altogether, the brotherhood provides the chelā with a continuous *satsang* (meaning literally 'community of truth'), which can be found in the company of holy men. The elders watch over the chelā's spiritual progress, encourage the good pupils and criticize, sometimes punish, the bad.

Within the community one is usually well aware of one's relative ascetic status, which to a large degree determines the patterns of

---

Opposite At initiation, these apprentice Nāgā Bābās had their heads shaven as the most visible sign of their rebirth into the brotherhood of Sādhus, in this case the Junā Ākhārā. Now they eagerly – and a little apprehensively – await the orders of the Guru.

Sukhdeva Dās and a guru-bhāī in a tender moment of mutual adoration. The guru-bhāī perfumed Sukhdeva Dās' beard and now adorns his head with a new cloth: acts of worship and love towards an elder brother. The Bābās are unaware it seems of their wooden 'chastity belts', uncomfortable instruments and symbols of sexual sublimation.

interaction. The Bābās higher up the hierarchy must be approached with the utmost deference and they in their turn may treat the young chelās with a certain condescension.

Ascetic status depends on age, duration of ascetic career, accomplishment and severity of austerities, and spiritual attainment. But complementing these rather self-evident factors is the elusive characteristic of 'charisma', and, certainly among Nāgās, not-so-elusive machismo. Displays of power and humility are both equally recognized as evidence of divine inspiration, but the various sects do have their preferences and their concomitant 'holiness ratings'. The Sādhu's rank in the organization may reinforce his prestige, but the rank itself is primarily determined by his ascetic status. As is the rule in all communities and organizations, rank and status are expressed in names and titles.

A Sādhu's name usually consists of two parts. The first is his 'own' name, which he received during initiation and which may be the name

There is a long history of enmity between devotees of Shiva and Vishnu, but at present this is largely a thing of the past. Although they camp separately at Kumbha Melās, friendly intersectarian contacts do take place, as is shown here by Mādho Dās (*left*), a Vaishnava, visiting the dhūnī of Mahesh Giri, a Shaiva.

Having taken the path to dedicate your life
towards gaining immortality,
May you know that the path that leads to it
is that of complete surrender and dedication.
Remember, you are the child of immortality.

Atharva Veda 15.17.10

A few kilometres away from the main festival grounds, Devrāha Bābā had a hut especially constructed for him by the government. A famous Bābā, he receives hundreds of visitors a day, including high-level politicians. He blesses a book containing his teachings, the essence of which is that in this Dark Age all ascetic endeavours are in vain and only Rāma-Nāma, the perpetual repetition of the Lord's name, may possibly lead to liberation. He lives very simply and is even naked, which is quite exceptional for a Vaishnava. He has left the body now, after having lived – so it is said – for three hundred years.

of a deity, a mythological person, a holy place or something with similar associations. It is carefully chosen by his Guru – a name is a kind of mantra as well – and should reflect certain characteristics of the disciple. These holy names have many levels of meaning and thus convey a cryptic message from the Guru, an indication of the disciple's position in the 'sacred life' and which way he should go. The second part of the name indicates his sectarian affiliation.

Commonly a Sādhu is not called by his name but addressed as 'Bābā', an endearing primal sound, meaning 'old wise man', which may be followed by the suffix 'jī', expressing respect. 'Mātājī' is the usual form of address for Sādhvīs, meaning 'revered mother'. A Bābā is often referred to as 'Sant', meaning of course 'saint'. More deferential is 'Mahārāja', that is 'great king', which is the usual form of address between Sādhus. They may also call each other 'Mahātmā', 'great soul'.

The majority of Sādhus belong to a sect or organization. Besides these organized Sādhus there is also a small but important group of independent Bābās, who follow the ancient tradition of solitary asceticism. They have usually been initiated by a Guru, but refuse sectarian membership on principle. Yogīs and Aghorīs in particular are found in this category.

Besides these real Sādhus and Yogīs there are some fake 'holy men' and to an outsider the difference between these groups is often not discernible. For instance, some beggars dress like Sādhus in order to increase their status and income; and criminals sometimes disguise themselves as Sādhus to escape the police, or to steal from Bābās and pilgrims. In small communities and villages fakes would soon be found out, but in the larger pilgrimage sites and during festivals they may score.

A Sādhu will not easily be fooled by disguises, but to make sure, he only has to ask a few seemingly innocent questions, which, however, contain a certain code to which only the real Sādhu can correctly respond.

The Way

For most Sādhus philosophy as an explicit, rational system of thought is not of much interest. They rather 'live' it, following the teachings of the scriptures – which are mostly mythological, but deal implicitly with philosophy or metaphysics – and the examples of Gurus and saints. In fact, the ascetic tradition can almost be called anti-intellectual; the rational mind is often seen as one of the obstacles on the path towards

---

Overleaf Right in the middle of the Kumbha Melā in Allahabad, Kālabāda Singh has set up his own shelter, where he receives pilgrims eager to have his darshan. For their benefit he magically invokes the deities, rattling the double-sided drum (damaru) and blowing the conch-shell (shankh). The visitors in their turn make small donations.

enlightenment. The mind is too much part of the conditioned world of appearances, which is not only 'unreal' and impermanent, but also the cause of suffering and sorrow in endless rebirths. Ascetics strive to change their perception of mundane reality, 'reprogramming' their mind and piercing the 'veil of illusion' (*māyā*) to experience the greater Reality behind it. The truth must be experienced rather than verbalized.

There are exceptions of course. These are usually found in the upper echelons of the ascetic hierarchy – the Āchāryas ('professors'), Swāmīs ('teachers') and Mahāmandaleshwars ('great leaders of a division, an Ākhārā') – who may approach the riddle of existence also from an intellectual, philosophical perspective.

> *Yogis, having abandoned attachment,*
> *perform action by the body, by the mind,*
> *by the Reason and even by the senses,*
> *only for the purification of the self.*[24]

As it is stated in this hymn, all the Sādhu's activities should be aimed at purification of the self. To this end, his life is thoroughly ritualized. Most of his time is taken up by performance of magico-religious rituals, worship of his tutelary deity, forms of yoga and meditation, and ascetic practices.

The self is burdened with karma, and purification starts with renunciation of action and particularly of the fruits of action. In order not to build up any more karma and even to try to reduce any residual karma from past lives, all action with a worldly motive should cease. Any remaining action must be done in service of the deity. Therefore even the Sādhu's regular mundane activities – sweeping the floor, taking a bath, cooking food and so on – must be conducted as rituals of worship.

> *As the burning fire reduces fuel to ashes, O Arjuna,*
> *so doth the fire of wisdom reduce all actions to ashes.*[25]

Right action, and thus renunciation, presupposes 'discrimination', the realization of the essential unity of the soul and the Absolute. This knowledge, this 'fire of wisdom', can be attained through yoga and meditation, through bhakti and the grace of the Lord. All these various components are interconnected in some kind of feedback mechanism, and although proficiency in one automatically leads to competence in the others, they should ideally be perfected simultaneously. But renunciation is the first, the fundamental requirement.

> *Living in temples or at the foot of trees,*
> *sleeping on the ground, wearing deerskin,*
> *renouncing all possessions and their enjoyment –*
> *to whom will not dispassion bring happiness?*[26]

Waiting for alms on the ghāt of the holy Shipra, the Bābās are not idle: this place is as good as any to give darshan, perform rituals, read, contemplate – or just to be.

Thus 'dispassion' is a key concept in the Sādhu's life, and it entails renunciation of the world of appearances, mundane pleasures, one's home, one's comforts, and the society of ordinary mortals.

Right Action
Renouncing the pleasures of the senses starts at the most practical, bodily level, the renunciation of 'all possessions and their enjoyment'. Thus the vow of poverty is absolutely essential for the ascetic. Sādhus may possess only the basic necessities for the maintenance of life and some paraphernalia for ritualistic use. Connected with this poverty is their striving for simplicity in the things they have to use, for instance their minimalism in clothing. Nakedness would, of course, best express the ascetic status of non-possession, but nowadays this is only practised by the happy few. The majority dress in simple unstitched pieces of cloth, some even in

rags, and some have a preference – which amongst tyāgīs has become an obligation – for natural products such as banana leaf and grass.

They do not work, do not 'produce' in a worldly sense and must depend for their livelihood on the gifts of devotees. This is quite easy when they are recognized as powerful holy men and donations keep coming in, but the less charismatic ones – though not necessarily less holy – have to beg. This is usually a passive form of begging, sitting in a spot where the faithful pass by, waiting for alms. The faithful regard it as their religious duty to support the Bābās and they know that begging is done out of ascetic principle.

Some sects go further in this principle and place limits on alms that may be accepted: for example, no money, only food; or no cooked food, only foodstuffs; or not soliciting alms from certain castes or on certain days. Some sects forbid active begging in any way, and some prescribe a certain form, as for instance the Gudār (see p. 44) and the yoke-carrying Rāmānandīs (see p. 65) If a Bābā receives more than he can instantly use, he should not keep the surplus for himself but either distribute it directly to his fellow Bābās and devotees, or contribute it to his organization. The various organizations in their turn run free-food places where they provide at least one meal a day not only for Sādhus but also for the poor.

One important source of bodily pleasures that must be totally renounced, is sexuality. Celibacy is the ascetic trait that is probably the least comprehensible to householders, who view sexual enjoyment as a right, even as a biological need, without which life would be quite mean-ingless. But celibacy follows logically from the ascetic's conviction that sexual energy can be sublimated into spiritual power and eventually into eternal bliss. It must be conserved, not squandered in fleeting encounters. Sādhus who start their ascetic career in their teens are lifelong celibates (brahmachārīs), which is considered the ideal.

One very well developed system dealing with sexual control and sub-limation, is hatha yoga. In its 'physiology', control is equated with retention and forcing 'up' of semen, and sublimation is the conversion of semen into *shakti*, the spiritual power that is the basis of all creation.

By rejecting sexuality the ascetic sets himself very much apart from society, for the emotional and social bonding it creates is thus avoided. Relations with women, wife and children, and familial duties would all stand in the way of the desired exclusive devotion to the deity. Celibacy thus causes a certain disinterestedness in social relations, a fundamental change in perception of one's fellow human beings.

Food, as another source of pleasure, must be limited to the bare minimum required for maintenance of the body. It should be taken as 'medicine' (real medicines should ideally not be taken at all) and it must be transubstantiated into prasād, 'divine food', by offering part of it to the fire and the gods. Practically all Sādhus are vegetarian, not only because of ahimsā, the principle of not causing harm to living creatures, but also

Right Living under a tree, the ideal home for those who aspire to renounce this world: preferably in the jungle, or on the bank of a holy river. The Yamuna once flowed right behind this tree, but is now barely discernible in the distance. A *tulsī* plant in front of the tree, protected by thorny branches against the ubiquitous and ever-hungry cows, sanctifies the place.

Below An exemplary place for a dwelling: on the edge of a town, even on the edge of the continent; moreover, in a sacred place, Dwarka, where Krishna once resided. The Bābā has built the hut himself, with stones appropriated from a nearby dam-construction site.

Overleaf Many temples and āshrams run facilities for itinerant sādhus, places to eat and to sleep. This open-sided hall in Ayodhya, the birthplace of Rāma, contains a few hundred lockers, where Bābās can safely store their few possessions, and in front of which they live – some already for tens of years.

because meat is polluting and supposedly increases sexual appetite. One meal a day must suffice and fasting is a regular occurrence, as are other restrictions in diet.

At the Foot of Trees

The security and comforts of a home one can call one's own must be given up. As it is prescribed, 'living in temples or at the foot of trees' is the ideal. And what is actually meant here, is a life of constant wandering without a fixed dwelling place, except for the four months of the rainy season. Many Sādhus, especially when they are young and adventurous, follow this ancient injunction of itinerancy and do not stay for more than a few days in one spot. Travelling light, either in small groups or on their own, they follow certain routes, making the rounds along holy places mythologically connected with their tutelary deity. In the past they used to walk all the way, but nowadays they take the train if possible, for they have the 'right' – in fact an old custom – to travel without a ticket.

At a monthly festival in Chitrakut – Lord Rāma's place of exile – pilgrims come to have darshan of the sacred mountain and the holy men. Touching the feet of Keshāwānanda Giri is a more direct way to receive his blessing, his spiritual energy. Modesty forbids these women to look at the naked Bābā directly.

One well known circumambulation consists of visiting the four holy corners of India: Badrinath in the north, Puri in the east, Rameshwaram in the south and Dwarka in the west. Another pilgrimage, especially suited for Shaivas, is to go up the Narmada river on one side to its source in Amarkantak and return on the other side, a journey that will take about two years to complete. Like migratory birds they move with the seasons, going south in winter and north – to the Himalayas – in summer, allowing for changes in this pattern when they have to visit important festivals.

After some years of itinerancy, however, the majority will find a place to settle, at least for a while. Apart from the trees and temples already mentioned in the hymn, the favourite places are a cave or a *kuti* ('hermitage') in the jungle, a hut on the cremation grounds, or a kuti on the banks of a holy river or on the edge of town. Characteristically, the Bābās do not own these places. They may live on territory owned by religious organizations, but quite a few are 'squatters' on public property, an ascetic privilege respected by age-old tradition. And just as characteristically, these places are either outside or on the edge of society, reflecting the ascetic's 'marginal' status. By giving up their own home, the Bābās claim the whole world as their home. Thus they may reside as 'kings' in their neat kutis, often in the most beautiful locations.

Perhaps the majority of Bābās lives semi-permanently in āshrams, of which there are thousands, in all sizes, everywhere. A life without mundane worries, with free food and shelter. These are the very old Bābās, the functionaries and the Mahants, the monk-type Sādhus and the scholars. Occasionally, however, they may have to go on pilgrimage or attend important religious festivals.

As a rule a Sādhu will settle down in a place that 'belongs' to his deity, or in a place sacred to all, such as Benares, Allahabad and Rishikesh. Typical Shaiva places are Hardwar, Ujjain, Nasik, Junagadh and Pashupatinath. Rāmānandīs favour places where Lord Rāma used to reside: Ayodhya, Chitrakut, Rameshwaram; and devotees of Krishna would ideally stay in Brindavan and Dwarka.

The primary motive for staying in these places is obviously their sacredness. These are power-spots where the deity in person has touched the earth, where somehow the divide between heaven and earth is more easily bridged. Moreover, in such locations there are many temples where one may worship the deity, as well as āshrams, where free food is available. And last but not least, there is a never-ending stream of pilgrims, who not only worship the deities in the temples but also visit the Bābās in the vicinity, thus providing them with a steady source of income.

Many Sādhus, especially those who have their own kuti, cave or tree, lead a rather solitary life, a consequence of the basically individualistic nature of asceticism. Except for the determined hermits who shun all contact with the outside world, most Sādhus are, however, quite sociable and hospitable. They visit each other regularly and receive guests – lay disciples and devotees, pilgrims and the merely curious – with royal generosity. Whatever has come their way in the form of food, drink and smoke, they will share with their visitors, without worries for the morrow.

Naturally, visitors have their duties too. Freeloading is not appreciated though it can never be entirely avoided. But there is a tacit agreement that the visitor, within his means, should contribute to the Sādhu's 'cornucopia', either in kind, in money, or in services. These donations are not meant to gratify the Bābā's ego or fill his purse, but they are – or should be – contributions to the common weal and ultimately offerings to the deity. It is as such that they are accepted.

Happiness

The main social function of the Bābā could be described as giving, radiating spiritual energy. This he may do by various methods. Some of the offerings he has received, such as fruits, sweets and flowers, will be sacrificed to the deity, some of them he will keep for himself, but most of them will be given back to the faithful. These items will now have become prasād, that is 'food from the gods', having been charged with spiritual energy by the touch of, or proximity to the Sādhu, which in this way is transmitted to the recipients. Ashes from his sacred fire are also distributed as prasād to be used for spiritual and medicinal purposes.

To look at a divine image is called 'having darshan', and through this perception spiritual energy is transferred. Sādhus 'give' darshan by allowing themselves to be looked at, and thus transmit their spiritual energy passively. For this to happen, the 'taker' of darshan must have the right attitude of adoration, respect and admiration. He must know that he is in the presence of a holy man, the representative of the deity, an ascetic who has renounced all earthly pleasures – in a way no ordinary mortal can do – in order to attain liberation, and not only for himself but for all. In his 'being' the Sādhu points the way; through him the divine light shines most clearly.

Giving darshan and prasād may be considered the principal methods of transferring spiritual energy, but there are others: the Bābā may breathe it into an object, like a flower, a vial of water, a pinch of ashes; or he may blow air directly at the devotee; he may sprinkle water from his long hair or beard in the direction of the devotee, or give him water that has run over his feet; he may pronounce a mantra over the devotee or whisper it into his ear; he may give his blessing (āshirvād), psychological advice and spiritual instructions; and he may hold public religious discourses. Finally, in his absence, he may give darshan telepathically to his disciples and close devotees, and through his image, his photo.

This energy transfer is not a wholly one-sided affair. The Sadhu is the 'director' and main 'performer', but the audience must contribute its energy in the form of attention and devotion.

A Nāgā Bābā distributes ash from his sacred fire as prasād, food from the gods, to the grateful pilgrims who have come to celebrate the four-day festival of Shiva-rātri (the 'night of Shiva'). A carefully kept treasure, this ash is taken home for later use, devotional or medicinal.

Visitors with too much bad karma, whose 'vibrations' are too negative, whose habits are too polluting, may be permitted a brief glance at the Bābā, just to have the benefits of darshan, but they are not allowed to stay in the sacred vicinity of the dhūnī where they might poison the atmosphere. After all, everybody is responsible for his own karma. A Bābā may take over a part of somebody else's karma and so help him on the way, but then the Bābā must suffer the consequences and has to work it out himself. The Sādhus are no soft-minded idealists who think they

can – or must – help anybody; rather they are streetwise realists who have accepted the fact that some individuals are beyond redemption.

'Living under a tree', that is without walls, has one obvious disadvantage: anybody can drop by and disturb the peace, or, worse, pollute this holy space. To preserve the purity and sanctity of his place, the Bābā enforces certain rules of conduct and creates boundaries, often invisible to the uninitiated, to mark off his domain and its holiest spots.

When entering this territory – as in temples – the visitor has to take off his shoes. He greets the Bābā respectfully, preferably with the salutation common in his sect, and awaits the gesture of the Bābā indicating the place where he may sit. He sits down on the ground, with folded legs, the feet nicely tucked away. The Bābā usually sits on the other side of the dhūnī on his *āsana*, his 'seat', which often doubles as bed. Consisting of several folded blankets and sometimes an animal skin, usually on a slightly elevated platform, it is a very private place. Only Sādhus will be invited to share it with him and the common visitor should take care not even to touch it. The immediate vicinity of the dhūnī and the sacred fire itself are of course off-limits, as are the altar and shrine.

Certainly if this is a first encounter, a donation would be appropriate; the magnitude of this offering should reflect the Bābā's status – and the visitor's. Money he can always use, but if he is a smoking Bābā, he would definitely prefer a good piece of *charas* (hashish). If he likes the visitor, the Bābā will offer him tea, food and smoke, and will entertain him with instructive stories and 'acts'. All attention should be directed at the Bābā; if he is powerful this will happen quite naturally.

In his 'kingdom' a Sādhu can do very much as he pleases. There is no authority to whom he has to answer, except his Guru. Individuality is pronounced, even though Sādhus, as members of a sect, wear its 'uniform'. Some Sādhus are very austere, others are more relaxed. Even the most saintly Bābās may display their tempers, cherish their quirks, have their 'acts'. They are very human – sometimes all too human – but they know when they falter, are aware of the watchful eye of the Divine Presence.

> *Let one practise concentration;*
> *or let one indulge in sense-enjoyment.*
> *Let one find pleasure in company; or in solitude.*
> *He alone is happy, happy, verily happy,*
> *whose mind revels in Brahman.*[27]

Opposite Mahant Rāmakewal Dās sits on his āsana, with his personal possessions and ritual objects in easy reach, strategically located in a corner of the main hall of his āshram, next to the Rāma-Sītā shrine. Here he receives his visitors.

5 Living Idols

The Hindus inhabit an enchanted land where the Divine makes its presence known in a multitude of forms: mountains, rocks, boulders, stones, oceans, rivers, lakes, wells, trees, plants, animals and human beings. As if this is not enough, the Divine manifests itself in 'self-created' and man-made sculptures and images, in hymns and in songs.

As long as direct perception of the Divine – supreme darshan – is not realized, which is the case for most mortals, to have darshan of the various divine manifestations will inspire the seeker, laity and Sādhu alike, and give a clue about the nature of the real Thing.

Perception is one side of the darshan process, worshipping the divine representation as 'idol' is the other. Through the rituals of worship the officiant establishes a relation with the divine 'in' the object. Simultaneously, with his devoted attention, he augments its spiritual energy. Idols can thus be considered as 'accumulators' and 'conductors' of spiritual energy.

The Sādhus can certainly be regarded as a special class of 'idols'. After all, in appearance and behaviour they most closely resemble the gods as they are known through popular mythology and iconography. Consequently the holy men are worshipped as 'living idols'.

Seemingly in contradiction with this veneration is a certain fear Indians have for these holy men – the 'bogeymen'. The Bābās have an age-old reputation as 'sorcerers' who may cast evil spells, a characteristic based on the 'false ascetic' in many popular folk tales, an echo of the outsider ascetic and witch doctor of old. Some Sādhus reinforce this fear by outrageous and provocative behaviour, again resembling mythological divinities, though only in their wrath or madness.

Icons
The Sādhus emulate the outward image of their personal deity, but, more importantly, they endeavour to internalize his being, his personality, his mind. By a symbolical – magical – metamorphosis of the body into a

---

Opposite In emulation of Lord Shiva, Nāgā Bābā Ānanda Giri wears his hair in long matted tresses. His big jatā must weigh several kilos and is thus not only a symbol of asceticism, but an ascetic practice as well. 'Big' jatā confers a certain status, but it is realized that it offers no guarantee for spiritual accomplishments. It may even inflate the ego and thus form an obstacle to realization.

divine 'vehicle', and by a ritual transformation of daily life into a sacred existence, they aspire to become like him and finally to merge in him.

Some Sādhus realize that their personal deity is 'only' an anthropomorphic projection of, or 'on', the Brahman, the impersonal, abstract, nameless god, and use him as a necessary aid to approach the otherwise unreachable Absolute.

Quite a few Sādhus, however, believe without question in the existence of their personal deity as the one and only true god, or as the most powerful one of the pantheon, out of whom the other gods and goddesses have emanated. They believe in his presence 'in' the idol, and in personal communication through their worship and his divine grace.

But then, in Hinduism it is no problem at all to entertain these different notions simultaneously; and the contradicting notions of materialism and even atheism can be included too. One may or may not believe in the Absolute and still worship a 'lesser' god, or even his idol: it is all the same, they are all true.

Not all Sādhus engage in outward emulation of their deity; some might even denounce it as useless imitation, which undoubtedly it sometimes is: the 'uniform' of the ascetic, without inner meaning. Nevertheless, in appearance and behaviour all Bābās distinguish themselves somehow from the populace, and from each other.

Since the Sādhu population is roughly divided into two camps, the devotees of Shiva and those of Vishnu, it can only be expected that the various characteristics of these gods are reflected in different rituals and symbols of the ascetics. But in fact the differences, which have been emphasized during the long-lasting rivalry of Shiva and Vishnu for supremacy in the pantheon, are mostly on the surface.

In essence the symbols and rituals reveal the common ascetic roots of all Sādhus, going back to the 'long-haired sage', the 'bearers of skulls', the 'horned god' and, beyond all, to the King of Yogīs, Shiva. One divine characteristic is adopted by practically all Sādhus: the deity does not work, he 'plays'. Thus the Bābās do not labour, they perform rituals. Many emulate Shiva's austerities, his aloofness from the world, his absorption in meditation, his ecstatic intoxication. Most follow his example as the destroyer of ignorance; and some follow him in his divine intoxication, his 'madness'.

The Body

The ascetic status is primarily exhibited in dress and body symbolism. The colour and design of a Sādhu's clothes are very distinct from those of the general populace. The most conspicuous are the shades of red, orange, saffron, ochre, pink – colours of the fire, the rising sun, the sacrificial blood, the earth – favoured by Shaivas, but worn by some Vaishnavas as well. Some Shaivas and Udasīn, but all Aghorīs, wear black, the colour of death (to the world), thus of renunciation. The majority of Vaishnavas

Bābās who continuously wear sackcloth (tāt) are designated as tātambarīs. Some wear only a loincloth, but with others, as is shown here by Mahant Rāma Nārāyana Dās, it has developed into a complete outfit that is only distantly related to the original 'rags'.

wear white or yellow, the colours of purity and surrender. Most Sādhus wear an unstitched piece of cotton cloth around the waist and a shawl over the shoulders; some wear a gown, a shirt, or a vest; but Bābās never wear trousers.

Some Bābās wear only natural materials, such as banana leaf, and some use the coarsest materials, such as sackcloth, which are not only symbols of asceticism, but mild austerities in themselves. A few wear rags, following a most ancient injunction, or, in a variation on this theme, patchwork clothes; and the Aghorī may use funeral shrouds pilfered from the cremation grounds.

Nakedness, in emulation of Lord Shiva, who is *digambar*, 'clad in sky' or 'the four directions', would of course best symbolize the ascetic status. It was this nakedness that particularly amazed the Greeks who first encountered India's ascetics in the third century BC and who called them 'gymnosophists', the 'naked philosophers'. It seems that in those times, and even until two centuries ago, the 'gymnosophists' were ubiquitous and could be found in most sects. Nowadays only the fully initiated Shaiva Nāgās can be completely naked; but usually they are naked only on special occasions, or in their own territory, and put on some cloth when

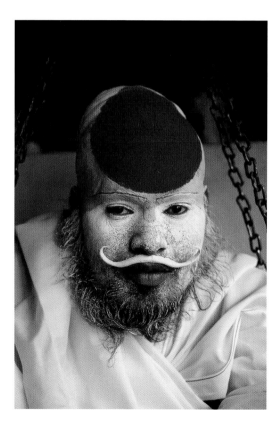

The basic Vaishnava design is still discernible in this elaborate, mask-like tilak with its enormous bindu, the Shrī-bindu, or 'seed of original creation' of the goddess Shrī.

they go outside.[28] In the past Vaishnava Nāgās were probably naked as well, but now they have to cover themselves with at least a tiny loincloth.

Nakedness sets the Sādhu apart from the populace at large, signifying his transcendence of attachments to the world. Since it is nakedness without any sensuality or shame, it is a clear sign of having transcended sexuality, of having attained a mental state reminiscent of the innocence of the small child. At the same time, being naked or semi-nude in all weathers is a severe austerity.

Almost all Sādhus paint marks of the deity, known as *tilak*, on the forehead and parts of the body. This is also done by the devout laity, when they visit a temple or after a holy bath, but they usually apply a simple speck or streak of colour to the forehead. As part of their daily make-up, Hindu women paste a dot between the eyebrows. The tilak of the Bābās is more elaborate and the painting itself, accompanied by the appropriate mantras, is a ritual meant to sanctify the body, to metamorphose the body into a 'vessel' fit to receive the divine power. In this ritual, tilak is applied to sacred objects as well, such as the 'prayer beads' (*mālā*), the water-pot (*kamandal*), the photo of the Guru – on his forehead of course – and the image of the deity.

Sects and even subsects can be recognized by the shape, the material and the colours of the tilak. The Shaivas paint three horizontal lines on the forehead with their fingers, using ashes from the sacred fire, sandalwood or other pigments, often dark yellow and orange. The three stripes are related to Shiva's trident, representing specifically the trinity of Shiva, Vishnu and Brahmā. Some Sādhus, following the ancient tradition to the letter, paint the tilak on other parts of the body as well: the arms, the chest, the back, the belly and the thighs. A red or black dot, the *bindu* – the 'void', the 'zero', the 'seed', also popularly interpreted as Shiva's third eye – may be painted somewhere between the three lines, or it may replace the full tilak.

The Vaishnava tilak, in contrast, is vertical. Two pigments are used, a white or light yellow clay, called *gopī-chandana* ('gopī-sandalwood paste'), which can only be found at Dwarka, Krishna's temporary residence; and a red pigment made from turmeric called *Shrī-chūrna*, meaning 'powder of Shrī'.

This tilak consists of three elements. Two lines are painted in a white or yellow 'U' form, starting from the bridge of the nose upwards to the hairline. The Rāmānandīs interpret the two lines as the footprints of Rāma, the imprints of dust from his lotus feet. The third element, a red vertical line or dot, is painted in between and represents Sītā. With the completion of the tilak, the goddess is united with her Lord, and the devotee is ready for his rituals of worship.

The multitude of Vaishnava sects and subsects have distinctive tilaks and sometimes different explanations of their symbolism. The Krishna devotees, for instance, interpret their tilak as Krishna's temple, housing

Brahmā and Shiva at either side of Krishna. Although the various designs are prescribed by tradition, individual variations are allowed.

Lord Shiva is the long-haired god, who uses his long, matted strands of hair, his powerful jatā, to temper the potentially catastrophic force of the river Ganges – the goddess Gangā descending from heaven. So it comes as no surprise that many Shaivas wear jatā, but many Vaishnavas do it as well. Long hair is an almost universal symbol of virility and strength, and Shiva's jatā are regarded as the 'seat' of his yogic powers. Jatā are thus a very distinctive ascetic emblem, suggesting possession of supernatural powers.

Nevertheless, many Bābās are clean-shaven, going to the other extreme of shaving off all 'five hairs': on the head, the cheeks, the chest, the armpits and the groin. As noted before, the Vaishnavas are an exception and always leave a small tuft of hair on the back of the head, the shikhā, 'like a flag of divine culture on the fortress of the human brain'.[29] Formerly the Bābās probably did not shave, for 'To save this trouble many sannyāsīs cause their disciples to pull out the hairs of their head and beard one by one'.[30]

The wearing of ashes, together with nakedness and jatā, completes the primal image of the ascetic as exemplified by Shiva and the 'long-haired sage' who is girdled with the wind and clad in brownish dust. Again, both Shaivas and Vaishnavas apply ashes if they choose to be naked or semi-nude, but only Shaivas use ashes for their tilak. These ashes are usually taken from their own sacred fires (*dhūnīs*) or from temple fires, but some sannyāsīs and all Aghorīs use ashes from cremation fires, the latter practice being the most ancient and magical, dating back to the times of the 'bearers of skulls' and their human sacrifices.

The sacred ashes, or *vibhūti*, are related to the fire sacrifice and are considered prasād, 'food' from the god of Fire. In the world of mortals, ashes connote death – 'dust to dust, ashes to ashes' – but for the ascetic, on the contrary, they symbolize immortality, the conquering of death, transformation and regeneration. The ascetic has 'died to this world' and sacrifices the self, burns his karma in the fire of austerity.

Implicitly, the shape of the body is also expressive of asceticism. The ideal, notably shown by the Nāgās and tyāgīs, is a supple, lean physique; a kind of boyish body, indicative of their pre- or rather non-sexual status.

While they are giving darshan, or performing their everyday chores around the dhūnī, Sādhus assume postures that are casual versions of the hatha yoga āsanas. The lotus posture, the padmāsana, is the ideal meditative pose; it 'centres' the body, aligns the subtle energy channels. As body language, it is expressive of the ascetic's life as a state of continuous meditation.

During ceremonial functions – and when they pose for photos – the Bābās tend to assume more 'official', rigid postures, together with various stylized positions of the hands, the mudrās. These mudrās are invariably

Like most Sādhus, Rāghunāth Bābā does not cover his entire body with ash, but uses it only for the tilak on forehead and arms. He has just painted fresh tilak after his bath in the holy Narmada at Omkareshwar and sits now in quiet contemplation, his hands in the tyāga-mudrā, the 'position of renunciation'. In this mudrā the index-finger (the ego) is under the thumb (the soul), thus symbolizing the desired ascetic state, in which the soul subjugates the ego.

The length of jatā indicates of course the number of years the Sādhu has engaged in his ascetic career, but not strictly so, for jatā must be cut when one's Guru dies. Evidently, these Nāgā Bābās have been Sādhu for quite a long time. Usually jatā is worn in a twisted bundle on top of the head and 'opened' only for special moments and rituals. After his bath an Udasīn Bābā (*above*) is drying his jatā in the evening sun.

shown in representations of the deities and express important characteristics of each particular deity.

The feet occupy a rather special position in the Sādhu's interaction with the world. The feet are regarded as excellent conductors of spiritual energy, which can be transferred by touching them. Thus it is not only submission when the devotee, taking darshan, prostrates himself and stretches out his hands towards the Bābā's feet and tries to touch them; it is for his own benefit. They are the one part of the body that can be exposed to someone else's touch almost without fear of being polluted. But not everybody is allowed to do so – some people are just too evil or dirty – and some Bābās simply do not like it.

With the feet one can also pick up energy from the earth, which is a good reason to walk barefoot in temples and in sacred areas. The most

Some Bābās wear ashes all the time, which is considered a mild austerity, and a distinction that sets them apart from those who do it only on special occasions. The Aughār Bābā (*left*) has smeared his body with wet ashes from his sacred fire. Krishna Jogī (*below*), an Aghorā Bābā, takes delight in rubbing his body with dry ashes – the remains of a cremation fire and, of course, the corpse.

Above Indrajit Purī performs a variant of the hatha yoga 'lotus posture'. His bright yellow egg-shaped 'third eye' and his body-painting of ashes are rather unusual and show a definite personal touch: the three stripes, though characteristic of a Shaiva, are painted in 'negative' as it were.

Overleaf Rāma Sāgara Dās raises his hand in the gesture of blessing, the abhaya-mudrā. This Bābā, who is said to be a hundred years old, has not moved from this spot, a small temple on a ghāt in Benares, for sixty years. Giving darshan, he wears a special mālā made of large pieces of tulsī, called *sūrya-mukhī*, 'mouth of the sun'.

compelling reason is to prevent defilement of the holy ground by shoes and sandals, which are considered most dirty unless they are the wooden sandals worn by some Sādhus – these are clean. Some wooden sandals, representing, for instance, a deceased Guru, are actually worshipped. The holy men can also transmit their energy to the earth. So where their feet have touched the ground, the faithful will gather sand and dust as prasād.

The disciple adores the feet of his Guru and will regard it as a privilege to massage them. When they are ceremonially washed, the water running off may be drunk as amrit, the nectar of immortality. Mythologically, this refers to the goddess Gangā, the Ganges, issuing forth from a toe of Vishnu, from where she falls down into Shiva's jatā. The references in the sacred literature to the Lord's Lotus Feet are innumerable and the images of the footprints of Vishnu and Rāma are worshipped as representing the deities.

Paraphernalia

According to the ancient ascetic traditions, a Sādhu should not own more than a staff, a water-pot, an animal skin as 'seat' (āsana) for meditation and some rags to cover the body. As noted earlier, nowadays Sādhus often possess more than these basic requirements, even 'luxury' items such as a watch or a transistor radio, but compared to the average householder, their worldly belongings are very few indeed. Some of these personal items serve a practical purpose – a blanket, a bag, fire-tongs – but most

The embroidered bag, or *jholī* – in this case adorned with an 'OM' sign – contains the Sādhu's few personal possessions, and is a symbol of ascetic status for both Vaishnavas and Shaivas, its small size indicative of their vow of poverty.

The trishūl is virtually venerated as Shiva's presence, 'dressed' with a piece of cloth and adorned with garlands of marigolds. It is the Sādhu's *axis mundi*, his 'spiritual antenna', establishing a connection between heaven and earth.

A primeval model of the trident is carried by Puna Giri: a stick with two antlers, which may well be related to the buffalo horns of the 'horned god'.

Clockwise from top left A brahma-pātra, a wooden kamandal, a brass kamandal and a dariye.

are exclusively used in rituals and are thus sacred objects that in the course of time have become emblematic of the ascetic status.

Foremost among these is the staff, or *danda*. It originated no doubt as a tool or weapon, but in a religious and mystical context it is the pastoral staff, the rod of divination, the magic wand, and thus a symbol of spiritual power. As the sceptre of sovereignty, the danda may only be carried by brāhman ascetics and is therefore far less frequently seen than other kinds of sticks – often weirdly twisted and knotted branches or roots – and weapon-like objects carried by most Bābās.

A very distinct weapon is the trident, the trishūl, the symbol par excellence of Shiva. Not all Shaivas carry it, but it is an absolute must for Nāgās. Apart from its symbolical function, it is potentially very dangerous: it is after all a lethal weapon. But Sādhus rarely wield it, and certainly not as they used to do until a century or so ago, in bloody fights against rival sects, the Muslims and the British. Nevertheless, it may still be used in self-defence and as such is a silent threat in the background, increasing a Bābā's worldly power. A few Nāgās carry swords reminiscent of their warrior past. The Vaishnava weapons, rarely carried, are the mace of Vishnu and Hanumān, and the battle-axe of Parashurāma.

A practical tool is the *chimtā*, the iron pair of tongs for tending the fire, which may, however, double as a weapon. It is also used as a musical instrument, as 'rattle-bones' for rhythmically accompanying songs. Both

Shaivas and Vaishnavas carry it, even those who do not keep a fire, and it has thus become another symbol of asceticism.

A staff and a weapon can be regarded as optional, but a water-pot, or *kamandal*, is an absolute necessity because no ritual can be performed without purifying water. Naturally, it serves a practical purpose too, containing water for drinking and for ablution of the body after answering the calls of nature. Therefore all Bābās carry a kamandal filled with water wherever they go. Usually a cup is kept in it as well, since drinking from somebody else's cup would be very polluting: spittle is regarded as an extremely defiling bodily excretion.

The most ancient kamandal, no doubt dating from the Stone Age, is a hollowed-out gourd. It is called *brahma-pātra*, meaning 'vessel of Brahman', and it is the one with which Shiva is usually depicted, although in his case it contains divine nectar rather than water. The later wooden and brass kamandals have been fashioned after this primeval model, giving them their distinct inwardly curved shape. Brahma-pātras are favoured by Vaishnavas, who generally prefer more natural products and therefore may use a cup fashioned from a coconut as well.

Shaivas generally use the brass kamandals, or even the modern stainless steel or aluminium water-pots with a lid. A totally different type of kamandal is the black wooden *dariye*, which has a spout, a handle and a lid, and which originated from large coconut vessels. This kamandal is used almost exclusively by virakta sannyāsīs.

As a ritual vessel and sacred object, the kamandal is cleaned every time a Sādhu takes a bath. The brahma-pātra is easiest to purify, a mantra suffices. The others have to be scoured with sand or ashes. The kamandal may be worshipped as well, by applying tilak on the outside and putting flowers in the water, thus transforming the water into amrit, nectar.

Practically all Sādhus wear strings of beads, or mālās, around the neck, sometimes around the arms, and more rarely still as a 'crown' (see p. 29). When worn, the mālā serves as a kind of amulet, offering protection against evil influences. Its primary function, however, is as 'prayer-beads'; the beads are counted while mantras are recited or the name of the deity is repeated. The usual number of beads on the mālā is 108, a holy number, but mālās of 50 and 1000 beads are also used.[31]

The Shaiva prayer beads are easily distinguished from those of the Vaishnavas: the former are *rudrāksh* piths, the latter are pieces of tulsī wood. Beads of rudrāksh, meaning 'eyes of Rudra' (who is the forerunner of Shiva) are said to be very powerful. They normally have five lines,

---

Overleaf As part of his meditations, Sādhu Charan recites mantras with the aid of a rudrāksh mālā, hidden in his mālā bag. According to hatha yoga 'physiology', the recitation of mantras produces vibrations in the 'subtle nerves', which in a kind of crystallization process transform these channels and improve their conductivity of spiritual energy.

A rudrāksh mālā, consisting of 108 beads, and a small tulsī mālā.

which are called 'mouths'. The beads are more powerful the further the number of 'mouths' deviates from the norm of five. Apart from this sect-specific mālā, mālās of crystal and amber – with its mysterious electric properties – are also used.

The Vaishnava mālās consist of tulsī beads. The sacred tulsī plant is a type of basil, which has medicinal and purifying properties. Lakshmī 'inhabits' the plant and every year, in an all-India festival, she, as plant, is married to Vishnu. Among Vaishnavas the use of the mālā is much more prevalent than among Shaivas, for many Vaishnavas regard *japa*, that is, the endless repetition of the Lord's name, as the only way to salvation (see pp. 88 and 128). These mālās often consist of a thousand beads and are carried around in a big bag.

The sacred thread, or *janeū*, may only be worn by the 'twice-born', the three upper castes, and its investiture implies a vow to abide by the Vedic rules of virtuous action. It consists of three times three threads, 'the perfect number nine, which is the esoteric number of Brahman, the unchanging Absolute'.[32] The janeū is worn over the left shoulder and should be treated with respect and care; when answering the calls of nature for instance, one must turn the thread around the right ear to prevent defilement.

At the time of initiation, the Shaiva sannyāsīs discard the janeū, as they renounce the world and thus caste and its distinctions. That, at any rate, is the ideal; in practice quite a few sannyāsīs continue to wear the sacred thread. The Vaishnavas, in theory, do not recognize caste

Shiromani Dās performs japa by counting the beads of his tulsī mālā in the green bag; with the 'clean' right hand of course, and excluding the index-finger – the 'ego'. As a result of this meditational use the mālā becomes loaded with spiritual energy. To prevent dissipation or pollution of the latter, the mālā is often kept in this special bag, called *go-mukhī*, that is, 'cow-mouth'.

distinctions, and all are entitled to wearing the janeū after initiation, even those who formerly belonged to a lower caste. The Vaishnavas hold the view that the janeū is an indispensable reminder of religious vows and that it can only be renounced once final liberation is achieved. Thus from their perspective the sannyāsīs arrogantly and prematurely claim perfection by rejecting the sacred thread.

Traditionally the Sādhu is exhorted to sit on an animal skin for meditation. Lord Shiva's 'seat', or āsana, is a tiger skin. It is not only a symbol of strength, but magically the tiger skin transfers its 'power' to the owner.

Moreover, because of its electrical properties the animal skin prevents the subtle energy, accumulated during meditation, from escaping into the ground. Of course the most powerful skins, such as those of tigers or lions, are preferable, but these animals are now almost extinct and in their place the skins of deer are recommended.

Performances

With their costumes, their make-up, their 'props' and their public appearances, the Sādhus in a sense resemble actors on a stage. Many Bābās show great artistry in painting their face, adorning their body, decorating their stage and performing their act. Some, undoubtedly, do not rise above the level of showmen, but most are serious performers with profound acts.

As emulators or artists of the divine, the Bābās endeavour to express the unearthly beauty of divinities, which is evident to everyone but iconoclasts and pure monists. The Bābās' idolatrous performances are both for the spiritual benefit of the public and for their own good, since their primary 'audience' is formed by the deities themselves. Therefore they play, or rather 'are', their role just as intensely when they are alone with their Lord.

The first performance of the day is the bath, for as the popular Indian saying goes, 'cleanliness is next to godliness'. It is not merely cleaning the body, it is cleansing the soul, preparing oneself for subsequent rituals, transforming oneself into a vehicle fit to receive the divine spirit.

Ideally bathing should be done in a sacred river, by submerging three times while uttering mantras. Then, scooping up water with joined hands, the Guru and the deities are invoked. If the Bābā wears ashes, fresh ones will be rubbed on the body after the bath, and clean garments will be put on. After returning to his kuti, he will paint tilak on his forehead and body, and perform more mundane purificatory rituals, such as sweeping the floor and applying a fresh layer of cow dung around the dhūnī.

Power of Sound

These and subsequent rituals have to be accompanied by the appropriate mantras. A ritual without mantras would be a meaningless procedure; it would have no effect, or even a contrary effect, for the language of mantras forms the core – one might even say the 'soul' – of the rite. This language is intelligible only to the initiated and they do their utmost to keep it this way.

Opposite Swāmī Ānanda Āshrama reverently arranges flowers on the linga. While performing this pūjā, he is accompanied by his danda. A staff is the ancient symbol of the Master, but the Shaiva *ek-danda* – the 'one-staff', in contrast with the Vaishnava tri-danda, the 'three-staff' – also points to a higher truth: 'there is only One', the Brahman.

Many mantras, however, have become available to the general public, foremost of which is 'OM'. This mantra is regarded as the primal sound, the sacred syllable and 'seed' of all mantras. It was issued by Shiva when he sang the five notes of the musical scale and rattled his two-sided drum, the damaru. It is thus the essence of time and creation, the phenomenal world being the materialization of this sound.

On another level, it is the sound representing the Absolute and simultaneously it is the sound-form of the individual soul. With mindful, continuous recitation of the mantra this relation is re-established. As it is said in the scriptures:[33]

> The goal which all the Vedas declare, which all austerities aim at,
> and which men desire when they lead a life of continence,
> I will tell you briefly: it is OM.
> This syllable OM is indeed Brahman. This syllable is the highest.
> Whosoever knows this syllable obtains all that he desires.

There are many more mantras. In fact, large sections of the sacred litera- ture are devoted to them, minutely detailing their various uses, such as invoking the gods, imploring their blessings, begging for rain, asking for a long life and demanding the destruction of enemies.

Mantras can also form a kind of prayer, a focusing of the mind on the deity, or rather a filling of the mind with the divine presence. This is done by many devote Vaishnavas, who continuously repeat (japa) the name of their tutelary deity. This may be 'Rāma', 'Shrī Rāma', 'Sītā-Rāma', 'Hare Krishna', etc.

At first japa will have to be done vocally, with the aid of a mālā to keep count of the number of recitations one has vowed to perform per day. After some practice, it should be done mentally, for this is consid- ered much more efficacious. Eventually japa will go on automatically, even during sleep, creating a 'key-tone' harmonizing all spiritual activity. There is another benefit of perpetual japa: pronouncing the deity's name at the moment of death guarantees a direct transport to heaven. So with perfected, automated japa one is always prepared.

The really powerful, personal mantra is imparted by the Guru, whis- pered in the disciple's ear, never to be repeated out loud, for when overheard it loses its power. With this mantra a telepathic bond is established and the Guru can be 'called up' whenever his guidance is needed. And, conversely, the Guru knows everything the disciple is thinking or doing.

Mantras can also be used as incantations for magical purposes – perhaps their primary, most ancient function. These may be for good or for bad: they can cure diseases and kill an enemy; they can exorcize ghosts or drive a man crazy. This is one of the reasons that many Indians harbour a certain fear of Sādhus: as masters of mantras they could be evil sorcerers, who in their anger might discharge destructive curses.

With total concentration this Bābā is reading the Rāmāyana, the great epic poem narrating the life of god–king Rāma. Memorizing, analyzing and absorbing the Rāmāyana is a lifelong pursuit for many Vaishnavas and some become professional, even famous, exegetes, reciting and interpreting the texts to the public. It is believed that hearing the sacred words is in itself liberating and will confer the grace of Rāma.

At sunset Rāmanāth Giri performs the 'twilight' worship. He adorns his dhūnī with fresh flowers and makes offerings to the sacred fire, 'feeding' it with pure foodstuffs, all the while reciting mantras. After his pūjā, Rāmanāth Giri rattles Shiva's two-sided drum, the damaru, by rapidly twisting his wrists. The two sides of the drum are struck by the attached balls of leather, producing high-pitched rhythms, which together with the Bābā's audible invocations of the deity fuse into one penetrating, reverberating overtone – a primal sound. The stack of cassette-tapes behind him might seem incongruous, but they all contain devotional songs. A clash – or blend – of cultures: the 'Stone Age' ascetic life and its magical rituals in this electronic age.

Worship

Apart from the rituals meant to sanctify their daily life, Bābās will devote much of their time to paying homage to their particular deity. This ritual of worship, called pūjā, was a pre-Vedic alternative to the brāhmanic fire sacrifice for communication with the deity. But pūjā came to include the use of fire as well – and vice versa – showing the synergetic tendencies of Hinduism.

Pūjā is 'essentially and originally…an invocation, reception and entertainment of the deity as a royal guest.'[34] This is most clearly demonstrated in the treatment of the doll-size lifelike statues of Rāma and Sītā, or Krishna and Rādhā, by their devotees. These idols of the divine

Left A fine collection of chilams: nothing fancy, but efficient tools. They are not really sacred objects, for too many people handle them, but some symbolism is still attached to the chilam: the clay pipe represents Shiva's body, the charas his 'mind', the smoke his divine effluence, the 'high' his prasād.

Below Nāgā Bābā Hari Giri disappears in clouds of smoke. Many times a day he smokes the chilam, a common yet sacred ritual integrated in his ascetic routine. Sādhus prefer smoking in company and the loud cry of the chilam-mantra not only draws the attention of the deity, it also attracts fellow-smokers. It is often done before or during the performance of austerities; in fact, smoking is considered an austerity in itself, demonstrating non-attachment to the body.

couple, often sculpted of white marble, occupy the central place in the temple and the devotee's home; they are woken up by softly ringing bells and by opening the curtains behind which they had been sleeping; they are bathed with consecrated water, clothed with the finest materials and adorned with fresh flowers; they are fed before the devotee himself takes food; incense is burned in front of them and they are entertained with devotional songs; and finally they are put to sleep by closing the curtain of the shrine. Even if a Bābā himself does not live under a roof, he still may build a house for the gods.

Devotees of Shiva, who are on the whole a little less devotional than Vaishnavas, focus their worship on the rather 'impersonal', aniconic representation of Shiva, his linga. In temples this worship may be very elaborate, but otherwise Sādhus usually bathe the linga with water, preferably from the Ganges, decorate it with flowers and burn incense around it.

The worship of an idol is not inconsistent with the deity's omnipresence: pūjā just serves to make him direct his special attention to the worshipper, to manifest himself to him. During *linga-pūjā* for instance, the devotee transcends the notion of the linga as a stone object, or even as the 'phallus' of the deity. Instead he focuses his attention on the linga as a throne, on which he must install Shiva in his crystalline, 'formless' aspect. Shiva thus being meditated upon appears as an oval sphere of light over the linga.

Sacred Fire

For those Sādhus who maintain a dhūnī, this sacred fire forms the centre round which their daily rituals and ascetic exercises are performed. In fact, it should be regarded as the Sādhu's 'home' and his 'temple'. More Shaivas than Vaishnavas keep a fire, notably the Nāgās, but in both groups less than fifty per cent are dhūnī-wālās, 'fellows with fire'.

A well-kept dhūnī is a work of art. The square, or sometimes round fire-pit is daily covered with a fresh layer of purifying cow-dung. The dhūnī is adorned with fresh flowers, usually marigolds, arranged around the rim of the pit, and its immediate surroundings are purified by sprinkling water. The Shaiva will plant his trishūl in or beside the fire-pit, thus connecting the dhūnī with the heavens, stick his chimtā in the ashes and put his kamandal on the rim. The Sādhu's āsana is always close to the dhūnī, so he can stoke the fire, boil his tea, cook his meal and perform pūjā while remaining seated.

Overleaf Saraswatī Giri, a real master at the damaru, is about to start his performance. He rattles two different-sized drums simultaneously, each at a different speed. It is an active form of meditation and performing it for any length of time requires great concentration and physical strength. The damaru is of pre-Vedic origin and has clear antecedents in the magical practices of shamans who attained ecstasy by rhythmical drumming. It is usually made of wood, sometimes of brass – or of two skulls.

'Householders', that is non-Sādhus, are invited to take part in the chilam-smoking ritual, the smoke being offered to them as prasād. Most participate, even if they would never otherwise smoke. As prasād they can, even must, accept it. Smoking is part of the darshan of this holy man, and sharing in his high can be an intense religious experience.

A minimal amount of fuel is used: two or three pieces of wood or a few cakes of cow-dung. It burns, or smoulders rather, very efficiently, with hardly any flames – but a lot of smoke. The dhūnī is kept very clean, no refuse is ever thrown into it. The white or grey ashes are regularly raked around the fire with the chimtā or the fingers and the fire-pit may resemble a miniature 'Zen garden'.

The dhūnī and its sacred ashes are obviously related to Shiva, the fiery god and ash-covered ascetic, who usurped many characteristics of the Fire god while ascending to the highest level of the pantheon. The dhūnī is thus a prime symbol of ascetic status, indicating self-sacrifice through the burning of one's karma, transformation in the fire of wisdom, and rebirth from the ashes.

As an object – or rather 'subject' – of worship, the fire is saluted with gestures of respect and the uttering of mantras. As an essential part of pūjā the fire is literally fed – it starts to crackle and the flames leap up – with a mixture of the purest ingredients including seeds, nuts, grains, sweets and *ghī* . This offering is again accompanied by the recitation of mantras, which are directed to the Fire god, one's tutelary deity and other gods.

A common ritual, preferably taking place around the dhūnī, is the smoking of a mixture of tobacco and charas (hashish) in a *chilam* (pipe). Although this undoubtedly serves the more earthly purpose of socializing with Sādhu-brothers and devotees, the smoking of charas is none the less regarded as a sacred act. Intoxication as a 'respected' method for self-realization, among Bābās at least, is related to the drinking of *soma*, the nectar of the gods, which is recommended in the Vedas as a sure means of attaining divine wisdom.

Mythologically charas is intimately connected with Shiva: he smokes it, he is perpetually intoxicated by it, he is the Lord of Charas. He is invoked before taking the first puff by shouting one of many chilam-mantras: 'Alakh!'; 'Bam Bam Bholanāth!'; 'Būm Shiva!' Bābās offer the smoke to him; they want to take part in his ecstasy, his higher vision of Reality. As a final gesture of devotion, a Sādhu may mark his forehead with the chilam-ashes, or even eat them, as prasād from Shiva. Charas may be used by Shaivas and Vaishnavas, but many Bābās do not smoke at all and may even condemn the habit as low-caste and counterproductive. Shiva is the patron deity of charas, so it is no coincidence that almost all dhūnī-wālās are smokers.

Since the dhūnī is the Sādhu's home as well as his personal temple, it is not only the focal point of his rituals, but also the centre around which much of his social life takes place. His fellow Bābās and his other guests are seated in a circle around the fire, where they eat, drink, smoke and talk. After cooking on the sacred fire, a few morsels of food or a few drops of tea are offered to it, and then the Bābā and his guests may eat and drink. The dhūnī can only be touched by Bābās and close disciples; objects should be passed around it, not over it. As with any sacred object, it would be very improper to turn one's back to the dhūnī, or to point at it with one's feet. These rules and others ritualize to a large extent the interaction around the dhūnī.

In this setting, on his own private stage, the powerful Bābā is the main actor and master of ceremonies. From behind his dhūnī he directs his chelās and 'groupies' – the devotee-servants and hangers-on – and sets them to work, while he himself entertains and instructs the guests with stories, jokes and his 'being'. The daily routines such as stoking the fire, preparing the chilam, boiling the tea or just moving about are done with undivided attention and artistry, and should be regarded as 'performances', as rituals of worship too. For in Sādhu-life worship and meditation are not separated from quotidian affairs but totally integrated, infusing them with the spirit of the divine.

Sādhus who do not keep a dhūnī and still want to perform some kind of fire pūjā may substitute a wick burning in clarified butter, a lighted candle or a smouldering stick of incense. Even the illumination of an electric light is saluted with a mantra as a distant cousin of the Fire god.

A slightly different use of fire is made in *ārtī*, the circular waving of a flame in front of an image of the deity. This morning and evening ceremony is widely performed throughout India, not only by Sādhus, but also by priests in temples and by lay devotees in their homes. Since it is essentially a worship of the deity's image, its performance is more pronounced amongst Vaishnavas.

The waving of the flames – wicks burning clarified butter in a brass container – is usually done in a group, with one officiant holding the lamp while the others bang loudly on bells, gongs and cymbals in a specific rhythm. Invoking the deity, Vaishnavas will blow the shankh and Shaivas will blow the *nāg-phani*, the 'cobra-mouthed' horn, or rattle the double-sided drum, the damaru. This is often followed by prolonged singing of devotional songs. Thereafter the participants will approach the image of the deity and salute it reverently. The flame is then offered to all and each in turn will hold his hands over it and pass the hands over the face and the head, thus transferring its sacred energy. Besides this prasād of fire, each will receive a few drops of holy water and some sweets.

In contrast with the frequent use of fire, symbolically, ritually and practically, the Sādhu's last act – the disposal of his dead body – generally involves the use of water: his corpse, weighted with a rock, is thrown into a sacred river. This might appear strange given that the normal Hindu procedure of disposal is purification by fire: cremation on the funeral pyre, but in fact the Sādhu's exceptional 'burial' follows quite logically from the notion that he is already purified, has burned his karma by a life of renunciation and austerities.

Some Bābās are buried in the earth. This might be a legacy from the ancient pre-Vedic days, since cremation was introduced by the Āryans, but then, this is no ordinary burial either. Seated upright in padmāsana the Bābā is lowered into the ground; the grave is filled with salt – a 'slow fire' – and a spike is driven through the cranium. These ceremonies are meant to guarantee the Bābā's immortality, for he is not regarded as really dead: he has merely left the body and has attained *samādhi*. This term, which usually signifies the state of enlightenment while alive, has thus become synonymous with death as another form of enlightenment. It is often miraculously demonstrated, according to the disciples, by the Bābā's non-decomposing body, which may even smell of roses. The memorial stone placed over the grave is also called samādhi. The samādhis of

---

Opposite High up in the icy Himalayas, but naked all the same, Bola Giri Nāgā Bābā blows the nāg-phanī, producing one piercing note. This serpentine horn is related to the cobra (*nāga*), the intimate companion of Lord Shiva, always coiled around his neck.

powerful Bābās often become objects of pūjā and pilgrimage, since his immortal spirit is still there.

Thus Sādhus do not die, they leave the body and join their deity. The Shaivas go to Mount Kailash in the Himalayas, the abode of Shiva, and the Vaishnavas to Mount Meru, Vishnu's paradise. However, even though they renounce worldly life, Bābās are not encouraged to hasten their departure. In the past, ritual suicide by fasting, drowning or self-immolation may have been recommended, but at present only those Bābās who feel that the end is approaching may deliberately undertake the 'Big Trip North', going on foot to the Himalayas, drinking only water till the body drops.

Festivals

The Kumbha Melā is undoubtedly the most important gathering in the lives of Sādhus. It is held in Allahabad, Ujjain, Hardwar and Nasik, in twelve-year cycles, alternating in such a way that about every three years a Kumbha Melā takes place. The twelve-year cycle is related to the movement of the planet Jupiter through the zodiac; when Jupiter enters Aquarius (Kumbha), the occasion is most auspicious.[35] The Melā's exact date is also determined by lunar cycles; but the final decision rests with the Nāgā Bābās, particularly the Junā Ākhārā.

The choice of these locations is based on a myth concerning a pot (*kumbha*) of divine nectar, over the possession of which a heavenly fight broke out. Four drops of nectar were spilled and fell on earth, sanctifying those places.

Allahabad, also known as Prāyāg, the 'Place of Sacrifice', where the holy Ganges is joined by the sacred Yamuna and the 'hidden', mythical Saraswatī, is the most auspicious place, and its Kumbha Melā is the most important. Tens of thousands of Sādhus, sannyāsīs, monks and other religious professionals gather here, alongside millions of pilgrims. The Kumbha Melās at Ujjain, Hardwar and Nasik are considered slightly less auspicious, but still attract an incredible number of people. They are an impressive demonstration of the unshakable faith of Hindus in the holy bath as a means to wash away one's sins and purify the soul.

The Melā lasts about a month and there are several important bathing days. The main event is the 'emperor's bath', when all Ākhārās

---

Opposite The saints come marching in. They enter the city and proceed to the Kumbha Melā grounds in grand processions, accompanied by brass bands playing popular devotional songs. The Mahants, like royalty, sit in howdahs on elephants; in chariots pulled by tractors, bullocks or disciples; and in jeeps or luxury cars. The rank and file Bābās walk on bare feet over the wet pavement – hosed by the city fire department – over a carpet of flowers showered on them like confetti by the expectant populace, who respectfully welcome the Bābās, have their darshan, receive their blessing and, if they are lucky, their prasād.

Above and opposite In the Kumbha Melā processions, the Sādhus are the heroes, the stars of the show, proudly wearing their garlands of marigolds. The most awe-inspiring are of course the Nāgās with their trishūls and weapons. Demonstrating their martial games and ascetic 'stunts', they slowly wind their way through the narrow streets and finally reach their camp on the other side of the city.

form processions to go to the right spot along the river, wanting to jump into the water when the divine planetary influences are most auspicious. During British rule orders of precedence were fixed, a little different for every Melā, so that all rival sects would be content. Generally speaking, however, the sannyāsīs go first, particularly the Nāgās.

A Melā is a very social occasion. Sādhus who have not seen each other in years meet again. The brotherhood is re-united and everybody enjoys the exponentially heightened spiritual atmosphere. Important decisions will be taken, Sādhus will be promoted in rank and thousands of novices will be initiated, most of them young boys but also some older men. Some Sādhus will undergo their second initiation, renew a vow, start a particular austerity or end it.

During the Kumbha Melā, each Ākhārā forms a kind of legislative body, called the Shambhu Panch, which is in fact the collective of assembled Sādhus. Perpetuating the ancient 'tribal' heritage of democratic council-rule, this collective elects an acting committee of eight Mahants,

The 'emperor's bath' is obviously a festive occasion; nevertheless, the bathing processions are rather sober affairs. The Nāgās of the Junā Ākhārā for instance take off all their ornaments, mālās and so on. Wearing only flower garlands, in rows of two, they proceed to the river.

Standing on the edge of the holy Shipra, after having offered the flower-garlands to the river, all Bābās await a signal and then jump in en masse. They can only take a few dips, sufficient though for the purifying and sanctifying effect to take place, as more Ākhārās – and millions of people – are impatiently waiting.

called the Shrī Panch. In the three to four-year interval between two Kumbha Melās the Shrī Panch controls by unanimous decisions all the affairs of the Ākhārā.

A specific Shaiva festival, held annually in January or February, is Shiva-rātri, the 'night of Shiva'. In a sense it is Shiva's 'birthday' and, befitting the 'moon' god, it is celebrated during the first night after New Moon, when the lunar crescent, 'Shiva's moon', is visible. On the day preceding the night of Shiva, all Sādhus fast; they will then stay awake the whole night. The actual ceremonies start at midnight and include extensive pūjā of the Shiva-linga, recitation of mantras, processions and a holy bath.

There are similarities to the Kumbha Melā, but everything is on a much smaller scale. 'Only' a hundred thousand or so pilgrims attend this Melā, which lasts three to four days. They will all have darshan of the idol in the main temple and of the hundreds, sometimes thousands of Bābās. It is held in a number of places sacred to Shiva, such as the four Kumbha Melā locations, and Benares, Junagadh (Gujarat), and Pashupatinath (near Kathmandu in Nepal).

After the holy bath fresh ashes are applied and the Bābās return to their camp.
Finally, when all the holy men – and women – have taken their bath, thus sanctifying
the sacred waters even more, the common people are allowed to take their dip.

Another predominantly Shaiva festival is Gangā-sāgara, which takes place in January, south of Calcutta where the Ganges (Gangā) flows into the ocean (*sāgara*).

Rāma-nomī, the birthday of Lord Rāma, the avatāra of the Sun god, is observed at noon on the ninth day after the New Moon of March–April. Ayodhya, his place of birth, is naturally the centre of the celebrations, and the multitudes of pilgrims will congregate there to take a holy dip in the Sarayu, to have darshan of Lord Rāma in the many temples and to have darshan of the thousands of Bābās. During the eight days preceding Rāma-nomī, the Rāmāyana is read in temples and public halls, plays involving children dressed up as Rāma and Sītā are performed, and Sakhīs dance for Rāma in the temples.

6 Inner Fire

Renunciation, thus deprivation, is the fundamental norm of the ascetic's life. Many Sādhus, however, in their desire to speed up the process of renunciation in order to reach enlightenment in this life rather than the next, practise austerities and mortifications.

This self-chastisement should not be seen as atonement or expiation of sin, nor is it caused in any way by feelings of guilt. It is not repentance – which is always implied in the Christian notion of asceticism – but rather a pragmatic manipulation of matter to free the indwelling spirit.

A key concept underlying austerities is *tapas*, a Sanskrit word that means 'inner heat', that is potential magical and spiritual energy. Tapas also covers the various techniques of augmenting this energy, thus asceticism. In Sādhu parlance the word *tapasyā* is used, or shortened in Hindi as *tap*, and an ascetic performing tapasyā is designated a *tapasvī*.

The 'inner fire' of tapas is related, and in a sense opposed, to the 'outer fire' of the fire sacrifice, as illustrated by the myth of Daksha's sacrifice, to which Shiva, the tapasvī par excellence, was not invited. The tapasvī internalizes the sacrificial fire; in fact, he becomes the sacrifice; he burns within, increases his inner heat and thus his spiritual power.

The Fire of Passion

Sexual energy, *kāma*, the fire of passion, is both the main potential source of tapas and at the same time it is its opposite. This is expressed in the myth of Shiva killing Kāma by the tapas-fuelled fire of his third eye when the cupid-god of desire tries to hit him with his arrow of lust – the heat of kāma – in order to annul his yogic power. In other words, the ascetic must sublimate and control his lust, for its enjoyment would diminish, even destroy his spiritual power.

As an aid to mental control of the fire of passion, physical restraint is employed. This may take the form of continuously worn 'chastity belts'. Vaishnavas especially have given a great deal of attention to this

---

Opposite A very striking symbol of extinguished sexuality is the multiple chain arbandh of Hanumān Dās. Carrying a heavy club – Hanumān's mace – over his shoulder, he leads a procession of tyāgīs (renouncers) on their way to a holy dip in the Shipra. A joyful occasion.

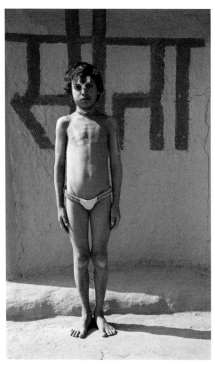

Left As a symbol of Sādhu status, the boy-Bābā wears the regular type of *arbandh*, a double rope; and a tightly drawn piece of cloth, the *langotī*.

Below left The wooden arbandh, as worn by Kathiya Baba (he is known by this nickname which is indicative of his tapasya), may quite rightly be called a 'chastity-belt'. Kathiya Baba started this heavy austerity seven years ago. And literally heavy it is: the arbandh weighs at least five kilos.

Below right On the sandy bank of the holy Sarayu, on their way to a bath, Angad Dās and Ranghare Dās pose with pleasure, the latter for the moment assuming a yogic posture. They have been wearing the metal chain arbandh for respectively seven and ten years. Their metal *langotīs* can be unhooked and are scoured with sand twice a day, but the arbandh stays on all the time.

Wearing this gigantic rope arbandh is not the only tapasyā Parashurāma Dās performs. As a khareshwarī he has been standing for eleven years and he is a 'non-speaker' and 'fruit-eater', too. The bandages cover sores, the result of standing. Nevertheless he is a cheerful Bābā, in high spirits one might say.

Hari Govinda Singh rubs earth on his penis, firmly ties the sling of cloth, stretches his legs and lifts the stones. It is a 'miracle' that the penis is not torn off. The scene recalls the chains used in the past to weigh down the penis continuously, but this exercise is now only occasionally done, and then for a minute or so. Just long enough to show the Bābā's power, his transcendence of sexuality.

type of 'underwear'. Consisting of a belt – the *arbandh* – and a loin-cloth (*langotī*), it is more than just a covering of the genitals. The belt's function as an instrument of sexual repression is made clear by the word arbandh, which means 'prevention belt'. The Shaivas, on the other hand, show their physical restraint by various 'exercises' with the penis.

The 'heat of digestion' is also manipulated for spiritual ends. Vegetarianism is the basic rule, but many Bābās eat only fruit and some live on milk only. Fasting is a regular practice and some Bābās will fast for weeks on end. It cleanses the body, sharpens the mind, and beyond a certain point induces 'weightlessness' and visions of the divine. Conversely, somebody who is divinely inspired does not need much food, he can 'live on air'.

A typically mental form of austerity is 'non-speaking', or *mauna*. It is meant to conserve mental energy, to still the mind, and to create social distance. It can be done for short periods as a kind of temporary mental retreat, or for years, usually twelve – a holy number, related to planetary cycles, representing one astrological phase of personal growth. The 'non-speaker', or *maunī*, may maintain absolute silence, or he may

Opposite These Bābās give darshan of their various penis-penances. The Bābā on the left wears a metal ring around his penis, an ornamental remnant of the large chains that in earlier times ascetics would drag along with their penises.

Nārāyana Dās, the Mahant of a large āshram in Ayodhya, is a renowned 'milk-drinker'. For over forty years, he has renounced the pleasures of food and taken no more than two glasses of milk a day. However, milk is more than just physical nourishment: as one of the five products of the sacred cow it is a spiritualizing substance. He practises another austerity as well: as a tātambarī, he wears only sackcloth and uses the same material for his bedding.

communicate through writing, or through gestures, 'hmm' sounds, snapping of fingers, etc.

A really severe mortification is the tapasyā of 'standing'. The *khareshwarīs*, who have made the vow to remain standing for at least twelve years, will never squat, sit or lie down; they sleep while standing. For rest they may lean on a stick or hang over a swing.

The tapasyā of keeping the right arm up – for twelve years or more – is even more mortifying and often leads to permanent physical damage. The arm withers away, it becomes a useless stick. Ascetics who practise this tapasyā are called *ek-bāhu* Bābās ('one-arm' Bābās). It has to be

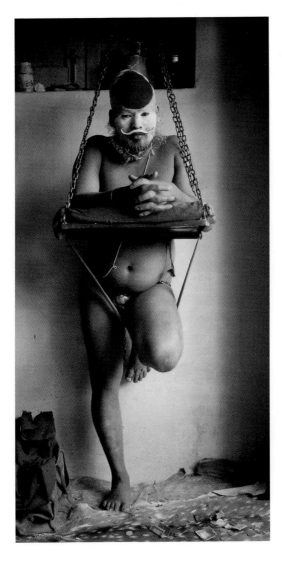

Bajrang Dās, a disciple of Bhagawān Dās (see p. 55), has stood for six years. He also wears a metal chastity belt, and is a 'non-speaker' and 'fruit-eater', too. Khareshwarīs may walk about, but they usually just hang on their swing in their corner – and stand.

completed by bringing the arm down. If this is not done properly, it may result in insanity, or death. Formerly there were ascetics who kept both arms raised (see pp. 24–25). These Bābās were totally helpless and had to be fed.

In these last two austerities the relation to the 'fire of passion' may not easily be established; but their successful execution involves superhuman willpower and certainly shows non-attachment to the body.

A much more active form of physical tapasyā is making a pilgrimage by prostrating the body 'like a stick' (dandavat), walking a few paces, stretching out again, and so on. One may also circumambulate in this way around a sacred object, for instance a mountain.

Some ascetics live in dark caves or underground cellars, never seeing the light of day. At the other extreme is the ascetic ideal, as prescribed in the holy scriptures, of never living under a roof. This is still followed by many Sādhus, notably the Vaishnava mahā-tyāgīs, who expose themselves indifferently to the vagaries of the weather.

A more deliberate use of the elements is made by ascetics who sit in a river with the cold water up to their chin and meditate for hours. This is done in winter. In extreme contrast, ascetics may surround themselves with fires, sitting in the bright and hot midday sun. This, of course, is done in summer.

The fire austerity is called panch-āgni-tapasyā, which alludes to the ancient practice, as mentioned in the scriptures, of surrounding oneself with four fires and taking the sun as the fifth fire. More recently it has been executed with varying numbers of fires, progressively increasing in the course of eighteen years. It is also referred to as dhūnī-tap, and it is obviously related to the sacred fire. In this ascetic ritual the Sādhu symbolically sacrifices himself to the fire: he has become the offering.

An ancient tapasyā, though rarely performed nowadays, is samādhi, usually meaning enlightenment, but in this case referring to a state of suspended animation, a virtual death that may last for a period of days or weeks, during which the spirit leaves the body and travels on the astral plane. The body stays behind, under the ground in a 'grave', but not in a sarcophagus as depicted on p. 24–25 – or in a casket under water.[37]

Within the Sādhu community opinion is divided over the efficacy and desirability of mortifications, especially those leading to permanent

Opposite Rāja Bihārī is just starting as a khareshwarī and has stood for 'only' five months so far. If a Bābā cannot keep it up, he would not be regarded as a failure, for no matter how short the period, he has at least exerted his willpower and reaped some benefits.

The austerity of 'standing', which is performed by both Shaivas and Vaishnavas, should ideally be performed under a tree, as is shown in the engraving on pp. 24–25. Indeed, the khareshwarī starts resembling a tree, especially his swollen feet, which look like roots with a firm grip on the ground.

Vasanta Giri (*left*) has been an ek-bāhu Bābā for twelve years now. Soon he may bring his arm down, but Amar Bhāratī (*right*) has at least still five years to go. Guided by an accomplished Guru, ek-bāhu Bābās gradually force the arm up and at first may support it with a crutch. This mortification can be executed in various degrees of excellence: the straighter the arm and the closer to the head, the better. Obviously, it is quite a handicap, the more so since everything has to be done with the left hand, the 'dirty' hand.

physical disability. Time and again renowned teachers have warned against extreme austerities, rejecting them as counterproductive. Nevertheless, they are still being practised after thousands of years, if less frequently and less extremely than before.

Teachers have emphasized that mental and spiritual renunciation are more important than bodily austerities, for only these lead to the state of real dispassion. Ideally mental renunciation should precede physical deprivations, but in practice it seems easier to begin by subjugating the body.

Mental renunciation entails casting off the ego, desires, conditioned attitudes and structures of perception. It 'essentially comprises the giving up of the ordinary conceptual way of seeing the world' and results in 'the break up of the conditioned mind and release from bondage'.[38]

Spiritual renunciation seems the hardest to attain. It requires giving up the pride resulting from intermediate spiritual accomplishments. Stronger than physical or mental attachments, this pride is the last and most tenacious hindrance to realization. It can only be conquered by sincere humility, the awareness that one always remains the humble servant of the great Master.

Circumambulating 'like a stick', the Bābā stretches out on the ground, places a stone in front of him, stands up, makes a few paces to the stone, stretches out again, and so on. This would be the 'fast' method, which is also performed by lay pilgrims, but Sādhus usually stand up and stretch out 108 times on one spot, simultaneously performing pūjā and reciting mantras. This way it would take two years to go around this particular sacred site, Mount Kamtanath in Chitrakut.

Above and opposite Preparing for his fire austerity, a Bābā sanctifies his body by applying tilak. Other preparations include: purifying the place with fresh cow-dung, taking a bath, arranging the heaps of fuel and the ritual paraphernalia, and making offerings to the fire. The first stage of the 'five-fire austerity' involves five heaps of smouldering cow-dung.

Overleaf In the following stages the number of fires increases to seven, twelve, eighty-four, and 'innumerable', until in the final stage a pot with fire is balanced on the head. Each stage is performed for three consecutive summers, so the complete cycle takes eighteen years.

The principal part of the austerity is the repetition of the Lord's name with the aid of a mālā hidden under a cloth. The final stage of the fire austerity is called *kapār-dhūnī*, that is the fire (dhūnī) in the bowl (kapār) on the skull (kapār). The circle of 'innumerable' fires around the Bābā is never completely closed, so the 'spirit' may leave – or the Lord enter.

Shiva Giri, a 'silent' Bābā, lives in this hut built of flotsam on the beach in Dwarka and takes care of five dogs and three rats. He practises yoga postures (āsanas) every day. Although most Sādhus have done so in the early stages of their ascetic career, it is certainly not a regular practice. Yoga exercises are not regarded as real austerities unless the postures, such as standing on the head, are maintained for hours. The āsanas mainly serve as a preparation for meditation by aligning the subtle energy centres and steadying the body. The fire austerity is usually concluded with the performance of some hatha yoga āsanas, particularly the 'head-stand' (*opposite*).

Enlightenment

Samādhi – but now in the sense of enlightenment rather than death – does it happen?

It is by definition impossible to judge the internal, subjective state of enlightenment by objective, external standards. Besides, it should be noted that enlightenment is not an all-or-nothing affair. It may dawn gradually, affording momentary glimpses, before a state of continuous self-realization is reached. Any external manifestation of miraculous or psychic powers would not constitute evidence of self-realization either.

According to popular opinion, 'real' saints do not exist any more, or if they did, they would not show themselves: they would live in inaccessible places in the jungle or the Himalayas, or in dark underground caves, or very inconspicuously amongst the populace.

Nevertheless, many Bābās do have a certain aura of sanctity and some have an all-India reputation for saintliness. Self-proclaimed saints being rather suspect, this is generally attributed to them by their disciples and devotees, who can cite numerous examples of saintly behaviour – love, humility, kindness, devotion, even 'madness' – and supernatural incidents, such as being in two places at the same time, preventing a train from departing, materializing objects, curing 'incurable' diseases, or reading the disciple's mind. Some famous saints attract enormous numbers of devotees without such miracles, but that in itself does not prove their enlightenment either.

Quite a few Sādhus may reach some kind of intermediate, 'saintly' level, but only a small minority may reach the pinnacle of true sainthood, however it is defined. Yet in this undertaking there are no losers; all are winners. For the 'results' do not, or should not, really matter; it is the endeavour that counts, following the way: to discover the inner light and let it shine, to make this life as holy as possible and enlighten the world, to follow the footsteps of the many who have braved the hardships – and enjoyed the rewards – of this radical, alternative way, in search of the Absolute.

The fire of penance purifies the soul,
Just as the flame of fire purifies gold;
the pure soul alone is worthy of exaltation.

Rig Veda 10.16.4

The Ganges, the divine mother Gaṅgā, links the Himalayas with the ocean, flowing
through Benares (*above and overleaf*) – better known among Sādhus as Kāshī,
the ancient name of Shiva's city, meaning 'City of Light' – and through Allahabad
(*opposite*) better known as Prāyāg, the 'Place of Sacrifice', where the brown Ganges,
just visible in front of the pontoon, is joined by the blue Yamuna and the 'hidden',
mythical Saraswatī. At these power-spots, 'crossover' points between heaven and
earth, the Sādhus gather and immerse themselves in Gaṅgā Mā, have her darshan
and disperse again, to wander across the land on their sacred journey.

Notes

1 R. Tagore, *Songs of Kabir*. New Delhi, 1985; III.26, p. 115.
2 S. Vidyalankar, *The Holy Vedas*. Delhi, 1983; Atharva Veda 10.8.37.
3 H.P. Sullivan, 'A Reexamination of the Religion of the Indus Civilization'. *History of Religions*. 1964, 4 (1), pp. 115–25. He suggests that the 'horned god' might be a female fertility deity. In his view the 'erect phallus' would be the tassel of the waistband.
4 J. Gonda, *Aspects of Early Vishnuism*. Utrecht, 1954; p. 11.
5 This eclectic rendition, following the spirit rather than the letter of the Rigvedic hymn 10.136, is based on material presented by K. Werner (ed.) in *The Yogi and the Mystic*. London, 1989; by H. Chakraborti in *Asceticism in Ancient India, in Brāhmanical, Buddhist. Jaina and Ājīvika Societies (from the Earliest Times to the Period of Śankarāchārya)*. Calcutta, 1973; and on oral information supplied by contemporary long-haired ones.
6 H. Omont (facsimile ed.), *Le Livre des Merveilles*. Paris, 1907; pl. 249.
7 G.S. Ghurye, *Indian Sādhus*. Bombay, 1964; p. 13: 'The description of one class of Vratyas in the Pañcaviṃsa-Brāhmana . . . as of reposing penis combined with the almost common representation of Śiva. . . with tumescent penis inclines us to the conclusion that the description of the "vātarasana" sages as "ūrdhvamanthino" refers to their characteristic achievement of keeping their penis tumescent without agitation or excitement.'
8 D.N. Lorenzen, *The Kāpālikas and Kālāmukhas: Two Lost Íaivite Sects*. Los Angeles, 1972; p. 21.
9 Ball, V.A. (ed.) *Travels in India by Jean Baptiste Tavernier*. London, 1889; p. 202.
10 Verse 2.28 of the Haravijaya by Rātnakara, in: D. Smith, 'Aspects of the symbolism of fire'. *Symbols in Art and Religion*. K. Werner (ed.), London, 1990; p. 141.
11 The Gurimallam *linga*.
12 I. Inderjit, *Science of Symbols*. New Delhi, 1978; p. 146.
13 The names and places of the twelve *jyotir-lingas* are: Somnath in Kathiawar (Gujarat); Mallikarjuna in Karnataka; Mahakaleshwar in Ujjain (M.P.); Omkareshwar near Indore (M.P.); Kedarnath north of Rishikesh (U.P.); Bhimashankar near Poona (Maharashtra); Triyambaknath near Nasik (Maharashtra); Baijnath in Bihar; Naganath near Ahmednagar in Maharashtra; Rameshwaram in Tamil Nadu; Ghrisneshwara at Ellora (Maharashtra); and Amarnath in Kashmir.
14 W.D. O'Flaherty, *Asceticism and Eroticism in the Mythology of Shiva*. London, 1973.
15 Chakraborti *op. cit.*; p. 186.
16 Mundaka Upanishad II. 1. 1., quoted in K.T. Behanan, *Yoga, a Scientific Evaluation*. New York, 1964; p. 22.
17 C. Sharma, *A Critical Survey of Indian Philosophy*. Delhi, 1979; p. 252.
18 Sadananda Giri. *Society and Sannyāsi, a History of the Dasanami Sannyāsis*. Varanasi, 1976; p. 22.
19 Aughāṛ in this sense is derived from an-ghaḍ or an-gaḍh, meaning 'unfinished, un-done, clumsy'.
20 A. Besant and Bhagavān Dās (transl.). *The Bhagavad-Gītā*. Delhi, 1986; II. 22, 31, 38; pp. 32–8.
21 B.S. Miller (transl.), *Lovesong of the Dark Lord: Jayadeva's Gītāgovinda*. New York, 1977; with slight alterations; I. 1, 25, 44; XII. 1, 10.
22 Besant *op. cit.*; V.7, p. 103.
23 Ghurye *op. cit.*; p. 180.
24 Besant *op. cit.*; V. 11, p. 94.
25 Besant *op. cit.*; IV. 37, p. 87.
26 T.M.P. Mahadevan, *The Hymns of Śankara*. New Delhi, 1986.; Bhaja Govindam 18, p. 62.
27 *Ibid*; Bhaja Govindam 19, p. 63.
28 Jain Digambar monks – perhaps totalling 500 in all of India – are the only contemporary ascetics who are naked all the time, everywhere.
29 Sharma Āchārya, Shrī Rāma. *The Great Science and Philosophy of Gāyatri*. Mathurā, 1991; p. 75.
30 Abbé J.A. Dubois, *Hindu Manners, Customs and Ceremonies*. New Delhi, 1983; p. 526. This is still done by contemporary Jain Digambars.
31 '108' occurs in various contexts. The many metaphysical and astrological concepts that can be divided into three, nine and twelve can be related 'mathematically' by this formula. For instance, the three 'worlds', the nine planets, the twelve signs of the zodiac, etc.
32 R.L. Gross, *A Study of the Sādhus of North India*. Berkeley, 1979; p. 511.
33 Katha Upanishad; 1.2.15–16, quoted by Chetanānanda, Swāmī (transl.). Avadhūta Gītā of Dattātreya: the Song of the Everfree. Calcutta, 1988; p. 90.
34 J. Gonda, *Vishnuism and Śaivism*, a Comparison. London, 1970; p. 77.
35 Each Kumbha Mela is to a certain extent characterized by the season in which it takes place. The ones in Allahabad and Hardwar are held in January or February and are thus 'cold' Melas; the one in Ujjain is 'hot', since it is in May; and the one in Nasik is 'wet', for it is in August during the monsoon.
36 Dubois *op. cit.*; p. 520.
37 A Japanese Sadhvī stayed under the ground for five days at the Kumbha Mela in Ujjain in 1992, and at the Kumbha Mela in Allahabad in 2001. This was observed by the author. Her Guru, Pilot Baba, who has performed this 'miracle' twenty-seven times, more recently stayed under water – without casket – for four days. Reported in the Times of India, 9 November 1992, he said: 'I have mastered the way to survive in conditions akin to that in the womb.' It is also reported that the Indian Rationalist Association accused him of fraud.
38 Gross *op. cit.*; 309, 310.

Bibliography

Basham. A.L. *The Wonder that was India.* London, 1967.

Behanan, K.T. *Yoga, a Scientific Evaluation.* New York, 1964.

Besant, A. and Bhagavān Dās (transl.). *The Bhagavad-Gītā.* Delhi, 1986.

Bhagat, M.G. *Ancient Indian Asceticism.* New Delhi, 1976.

Bhardwaj, S.M. *Hindu Places of Pilgrimage in India.* Berkeley, 1973.

Briggs, G.W. *Gorakhnāth and the Kānphatā Yogīs.* Delhi, 1973.

Burghart, R. *Indian Religion.* London, 1985.

Burghart, R. 'Wandering Ascetics of the Rāmanandī sect'. *History of Religions*, vol. 22, 361–380. 1983.

Burghart, R. 'Secret vocabularies of the "Great Renouncers" of the Rāmanandī sect'. In *Early Hindu Devotional Literature*, pp. 17–31. 1980.

Burghart, R. 'The Founding of the Rāmanandī sect'. *Ethnohistory* 25, pp. 121–139. 1978.

Campbell, J. *The Masks of God: Oriental Mythology.* London, 1962.

Chakraborti, H. *Asceticism in Ancient India, in Brāhmanical, Buddhist, Jaina and Ājīvika Societies (from the Earliest Times to the Period of Śankarāchārya).* Calcutta, 1973.

Chetanānanda, Swāmī (transl.). *Avadhūta Gītā of Dattātreya: the Song of the Everfree.* Calcutta, 1988.

Daniélou, A. *L'érotisme divinisé.* Paris, 1962.

Dimock, E.C. *The Place of the Hidden Moon, Erotic Mysticism in the Vaishnava-Sahajiya Cult of Bengal.* Chicago, 1966.

Dubois, Abbé J.A. *Hindu Manners, Customs and Ceremonies.* New Delhi, 1983 (reprint of the 1906 [1897] translation by H.K. Beauchamp).

Eck, D.L. *Banaras, City of Light.* London, 1983.

Eliade, M. Yoga, *Immortality and Freedom.* Princeton, 1969.

Entwistle, A.W. 'Vaishnava Tilakas'. *IAVRI bulletin* 11 and 12. London, 1982.

Entwistle, A.W. *Braj: Centre of Krishna Pilgrimage.* Groningen, 1987.

Ghurye, G.S. *Indian Sādhus.* Bombay, 1964.

Gonda, J. *Aspects of Early Vishnuism.* Utrecht, 1954.

Gonda, J. *Vishnuism and Śaivism, a Comparison.* London, 1970.

Gonda, J. 'Ascetics and Courtesans'. *The Adyar Library Bulletin* 25, pp. 78–102. 1961.

Gopinatha Rao, T.A. *Elements of Hindu Iconography.* Repr. New York, 1968.

Gross, R.L. *A Study of the Sādhus of North India.* Berkeley, 1979.

Growse, F.S. *The Rāmāyana of Tulasīdāsa.* Delhi, 1987.

Inderjit, I. *Science of Symbols.* New Delhi, 1978.

Isacco, E. *Krishna, the Divine Lover.* London, 1982.

Iyengar, B.K.S. *Light on Yoga.* New York, 1977.

Jansen, M. *Die Indus-Zivilisation.* Cologne, 1986.

Kinsley, D. 'Through the looking glass: Divine Madness in the Hindu Religious Tradition'. *History of Religions*, vol. 13(4), pp. 270–305. May 1974.

Kumar, S. *The Vision of Kabir.* Ontario, 1984.

Lorenzen, D.N. *The Kāpālikas and Kālāmukhas: Two Lost Śaivite Sects.* Los Angeles, 1972.

Mahadevan, T.M.P. *The Hymns of Śankara.* New Delhi, 1986.

Miller, B.S. (transl.) *Lovesong of the Dark Lord: Jayadeva's Gītāgovinda.* New York, 1977.

Mitter, P. *Much Maligned Monsters.* London, 1977.

Mookerjee, A. and M. Khanna. *The Tantric Way.* Thames & Hudson, London, 1977.

Morinis, E.A. *Pilgrimage in the Hindu Tradition.* Oxford, 1984.

Mukherji, S.K. *Psychology of Image Worship of the Hindus.* Calcutta, c. 1947.

O'Flaherty, W.D. *Asceticism and Eroticism in the Mythology of Shiva.* London, 1973.

O'Flaherty, W.D. *Sexual Metaphors and Animal Symbolism in Indian Mythology.* Delhi, 1981.

O'Flaherty, W.D. *Women, Androgynes and Other Mythical Beasts.* Chicago, 1980.

O'Flaherty, W.D. 'The Symbolism of Ashes in the Mythology of Śiva'. *Purāna* XIII, 1, pp. 26–35. 1971.

O'Flaherty, W.D. 'The Symbolism of the Third Eye of Śiva in the Purānas'. *Purāna* XI, 2, pp. 26–35. 1969.

Omont, H. (facsimile ed.) *Le Livre des Merveilles.* Paris, 1907.

Parry, J.P. 'The Aghorī Ascetics of Benares'. *Indian Religion.* Burghart, R. and A. Cantlie (ed.). London, 1985.

Picart, B. *Cérémonies et coutumes religieuses de tous les peuples du monde.* Amsterdam, 1723–43.

Roebuck, V.J. 'Weapons as Symbols in Hindu art'. *Symbols in Art and Religion.* Werner, K (ed.). London, 1990.

Sedlar, J.W. *India and the Greek World.* Totawa, N.J., USA, 1980.

Siegel, L. *Sacred and Profane Dimensions of Love in Indian Traditions as Exemplified in the Gītāgovinda of Jayadeva.* Delhi, 1978.

Sinha, S. & B. Saraswatī. *Ascetics of Kāshī.* Varanasi, 1978.

Sharma Āchārya, Shrī Rāma. *The Great Science and Philosophy of Gāyatri.* Mathura, 1991.

Sharma, C. *A Critical Survey of Indian Philosophy.* Delhi, 1979.

Skurzak, L. *Études sur l'origine de l'ascétisme Indien.* Wroclaw, 1948.

Smith, D. 'Aspects of the Symbolism of Fire'. *Symbols in Art and Religion.* Werner, K. (ed.). London, 1990.

Spratt, P. *Hindu Culture and Personality, a Psycho-analytic Study.* Bombay, 1966.

Staal, F. *Agni, the Vedic Ritual of the Fire Altar.* Berkeley, 1983.

Sullivan, H.D. 'A Reexamination of the Religion of the Indus Civilization'. *History of Religions.* 4 (1): 115–125. 1964.

Tagore, R. *Songs of Kabir.* New Delhi, 1985.

Tavernier, J.B. *Les six voyages de Jean-Baptiste Tavernier.* Paris, 1676. Ball, V.A. *Travels in India by Jean Baptiste Tavernier.* London, 1889.

Thiel-Horstmann, M. 'On the Dual Identity of Nāgās'. *Devotion Divine.* Paris, 1991.

Thomas, P. *Festivals and Holidays of India.* Bombay, 1971.

Tripathi, B.D. *Sādhus of India.* Bombay, 1978.

Unbescheid, G. *Kanphātā.* Wiesbaden, 1980.

Vasudevāchārya, Swāmī. *A Teacher, not a Preacher.* Ayodhya, 1990.

Veer, P.T. van der. *Gods on Earth.* Groningen, 1986.

Vidyalankar, S. *The Holy Vedas.* Delhi, 1983.

Werner, K. (ed.). *The Yogi and the Mystic.* London, 1989.

Werner, K. (ed.). *Symbols in Art and Religion.* London, 1990.

Wheeler, M. *The Indus Civilization.* Cambridge, 1968.

Pronunciation

The pronunciation of Hindi and Devanagari words has been indicated with a minimum of diacritical marks: only the long vowels have been marked with a horizontal line above them, except in topographical names, which are spelled according to conventional usage. In general, Hindi pronunciation has been followed. The accent is usually placed on the syllable containing a long vowel, or a syllable with a short vowel followed by two consonants, or on the first syllable.

Short vowels

a at the end of a word is not pronounced, or with a barely audible 'uh' sound; for instance Krishna, Mahābhārata, Rāmāyana, hatha yoga, should be pronounced as Krshn(uh), Mahābhārat(uh), Rāmāyan(uh), and hath(uh)-yog(uh), respectively.

    a as in car or as in arrive (but never as in cat).

    i as in pit

    u as in bull

    ai as in egg

Long vowels

    ā as in America

    ī as in machine

    ū as in rule

    e as in cable

    o as in go or sometimes as in more

    au as in cow

Consonants

These are roughly identical to the English consonants, but in the aspirated consonants – those with an 'h' – the 'h' must be distinctly audible. For example the th and the ph should be pronounced as in hothouse and shepherd.

When a consonant is doubled, the pronunciation should reflect this, as for instance in sannyāsī, which should be pronounced as san-nyāsī.

Names of Sādhus portrayed in the photographs (where known)

All photographs are by the author except for that on p. 10, which is by Manfred Pelz.

(l)=left; (c)=centre; (r)=right; (a)=above; (b)=below.

2. Mādhav Dās. 4–5. Prayāg Giri. 8. Saraswatī Giri. 15. Rupa Nāth. 26. Sukh Deva. 29. Shiv Nārāyana Giri. 30. Rāmeshwar Giri. 33. Saraswatī Giri. 34. Sādhu Charan. 35. Rāma Samundar Giri. 36–37. Lakshmī Nārāyana Giri. 39. (r) Mast Giri. 41. Sobhna Giri. 42. Darshan Giri. 45. Dishāma Nāth Jogī. 46 Desarat Rāma. 49. Gaurī Shankar Mishra. 50. Misri Dās. 51. (l) Nirvāna Rāma Dās & Ananda Rāma Dās. 52. (l) Rāma Dās & Govinda Dās. 55. Bhagawān Dās. 56. Hanumān Hari Dās. 57 (a) Rāma Chandra Dās; (b) Rāma Krishan Dās. 59. Sunmarpan Dās. 62. Hanumān Dās. 66. Mathurā Dās. 69. Gyān Dās. 70. Rāmeshwarānanda. 71. Umesh Dās. 72. Janaki Jivan Sharan. 73. Rāma Brahmadeo Sharan. 74. Jhunjhunia Bābā. 76. Premalātha Sakhī. 78. Parashurāma Bhāratī. 81. Tyāgī Bābā. 86. Sukhdeva Dās. 87. Mādho Dās & Mahesh Giri. 90–91. Kālabāda Singh. 88. Devrāha Bābā. 95 (b) Sādhu Charan. 96–97. Vishnu Charan Dās. 98. Keshāwānanda Giri. 102. Rāmakewal Dās. 104. Ānanda Giri. 107. Rāma Nārāyana Dās. 108. Bajrang Dās. 111. Rāghunāth Bābā. 112. (l) Rāma Giri & Sundar Giri; (r) Harbant Purī. 114. (b) Krishna Jogī. 115. Indrajit Purī. 116–17. Rāma Sāgara Dās. 119. Puna Giri. 122–23. Sādhu Charan. 125. Shiromani Dās. 126. Ānanda Āshrama. 130 and 131. Rāmanāth Giri. 132. Hari Giri. 134–35. Saraswatī Giri. 139. Bola Giri. 140. Shivendra Purī. 148. Hanumān Dās. 150. (a) Dhāru Dās; (l) Rādhā Dās; (r) Angad Dās & Ranghare Dās. 151. Parashurāma Dās. 152. Satyanārāyana Giri. 153. Hari Govinda Singh. 154. Nārāyana Dās. 155. Bajrang Dās. 157. Rāja Biharī. 158. (l) Vasanta Giri; (r) Amar Bhāratī. 160. (b) Rāma Charan Dās. 164. Shiva Giri. 166. Shayam Giri. 167. Dhānush Giri.

Index